SB

22

THE LITTLE GARDENER: BY J. S. COPLEY, R.A.

22

The Saturday Book

EDITED BY JOHN HADFIELD

New York
The Macmillan Company

THE SATURDAY BOOK was founded in 1941 by Leonard Russell and has been edited since 1952 by John Hadfield. This twenty-second annual issue was made and printed in Great Britain at Tiptree, Essex, by The Anchor Press, Ltd, and was bound by Webb, Son & Company Ltd, London.

Printed in Great Britain

Introduction

LAST YEAR *The Saturday Book* came of age, and we celebrated the occasion with a bumper number containing some
searching retrospections over the previous twenty-one years.
It was, we like to think, a substantial and enlightening series
of appraisals, and we were hardly surprised when—despite an
increase in our print number—we rattled out of stock before
the end of November.

But that is the kind of *Saturday Book* we intend to produce
only once (unless, as a quavering octogenarian, we are
recalled from Mon Repos, Bognor Regis, to assist in the
celebration of the half-century). With this, the twenty-second
number, we gaily cast off all necessity for *pièces d'occasion*
and revert to the quintessential *Saturday* formula, which, as
our constant customers realize by now, is in fact a total lack
of formulae.

'However do you think of all these things?' It's a frequent
and understandable reaction to a Contents List which is apt
to embrace (as this year's does) *art nouveau* and Horace de
Vere Cole, cast-iron conceits in South African architecture,
Edwardian nudes, and the mythology of the salamander.
The answer is, of course, that we don't *think* of them: they
just come to mind. Their journey from the recesses of the
Unconscious to the editorial drawing-board is prompted
almost always by Chance.

For instance, we had long admired the wood-engravings of
that canal-boat enthusiast, John O'Connor. We had been
corresponding for a year or two with Miss Picton-Seymour,
whose loving and elegant architectural studies have not
hitherto had much circulation outside South Africa. We had
been corresponding, too, with Mr Maass of Philadelphia,
who has a Betjeman-like devotion to nineteenth-century
American buildings. It was not until we were standing in just
such a building—the last of the original houses in Lexington
Avenue still to be entirely occupied as a private residence—
that the formula for a Summit Meeting between Messrs
O'Connor and Maass and Miss Picton-Seymour crystallized
in our mind. We were looking at the Tiffany glass lampshades

which preside over every curiosity-laden table in Mr Leo Lerman's treasure house when we realized we had never given *l'Art Nouveau* the *Saturday* treatment.

A symposium of styles! Why, of course! *L'Art Nouveau*—and who better to write about it than Barbara Morris of the V. & A.—South African Rococo—American Gothic—Canal-Boat Baroque—and we'd ask Olive Cook and Edwin Smith to throw in some documentation on English Suburban as well. What could be simpler, more logical, and—to our own taste—more delightful and instructive?

So that's how that happened—and our thanks to you, Mr Lerman, in your Lexington Avenue mansion, for unwittingly shaping about half the contents of this year's issue.

But . . . the other half? Well, we admit it isn't quite so easy to account for the juxtaposition of Horace de Vere Cole and the Siamese Twins, the Gold Rush and the Art of Duelling, Twm Shon Catti (we'd never heard of *him* before; had you?) and Mr Schenk's 'Draperies'.

Alas! It would take us all the 288 pages of this book to trace, substantiate, and (still more) justify by logical argument the emergence of these themes from the waking dreams of early Monday morning to the clear proof-read pages of *Saturday* noon. We would rather use the remaining 286 pages to better effect.

When one of the earlier *Saturday Books* was chosen (as several have been) by the National Book League as an outstanding example of book design the contents were described by one of the adjudicators as a 'mish-mash'. Let us content ourselves with the simple statement that here is the 'mish-mash' as before. We have mished and we have mashed, and we hope you will find some amusement and instruction in the result. Whatever faults or failings this year's *S.B.* may have it is at least, in our view, wholly *Saturdiurnal*.

J.H.

P.S. Yes, the editorial peacock is still fit and well. At the moment of going to press he has two wives and eight chicks, all, as it happens, hatched on a Saturday.

Contents

SB

22

The Changing Face of Childhood

The Changing Face of Childhood

BY MADGE GARLAND

IT IS inevitable that any conception of childhood must be a false one, since it cannot be conceived by the child itself, but only by the adult when he has really forgotten his own childhood and can only imagine what he remembers. Therefore every individual and each age sees the child from a different viewpoint. Sometimes considered an imp of Satan, at another a gift of God, alternating between the Low Church's view of original sin and Rousseau's belief in original innocence, the child has represented opposite ways of thought and appeared in many varied aspects.

At first an object of complicated fertility rites, later almost ignored by great civilizations of the past which have left remarkably few child portraits (that of Nefertiti's daughters is a delightful exception), the child first enters art in classical mythology as Eros, symbol of sexual love, but does not become a popular subject until the triumph of Christianity in the West. From then until now artists have delighted in capturing the fleeting and changing attitudes of children— always with widely different results. The Holy Child of the early icons seems to belong to a totally different species from the lovely, laughing children of Reynolds; the splendid young aristocrats of Van Dyck or Velasquez bear little relation to the untidy proletarians of today; the pale, rickety babes of the Flemish masters are no forerunners of the rosy cherubs of Boucher and Fragonard, and who would suppose that the not-so-distant descendants of Kate Greenaway's carefree boys and girls would lie upon the psycho-analyst's couch?

The age of innocence illumined with intimations of immortality has become the ante-room of Freud's young libertines, and a nursery (when it exists) is no longer the palace of a sheltered 'Small Person' but a nest for neurotics.

Water-colour drawing by Berthe Morisot of Madame Pontillon and
her daughter, *c.* 1872, now in the collection of Mrs Mellon Bruce

AMONG the varied results of substituting a brisk young girl or an even younger mother, both versed in the latest theories of upbringing, for a comfy but ignorant nanny, is that no veneer of good manners or best clothes hides the essential child from the artist today, and the uncombed youngsters of Buffet's and Bratby's brushes have replaced the freshly washed darlings of the past. The outmoded sense of sin has been superseded by the present fear of repressions which might blight the child's future, but the vanity which was once considered venal is now eagerly welcomed by mothers whose daughters can (with difficulty) be distinguished from their brothers.

It is unlikely that either sex today would be persuaded to wear their hair in the manner of the young Spanish prince on the left, but little girls still preen themselves in the mirror, reflecting through the years the happiness experienced at their own image.

Above: Detail of a portrait of a young Spanish prince dressed as a cardinal, by Juan Batista Martinez, Toledo Museum of Art, U.S.A.

Opposite: Getting ready for school, by Dora Holzhandler, from the Portal Gallery

La Toilette, by Chardin, National Gallery, Stockholm

THE CHILD'S early connection with fertility survives in such relics of ancient folk-lore as the straw dollies still made at harvest time in some parts of the country. In ancient days, when multiple reproduction spelt survival, not a housing or food problem, fertility was of prime importance and was worshipped under many aspects. One of the earliest known examples of the mother-and-child theme is the Cycladic statuette of a woman carrying a child, shown on the right. The strangely shaped barrel figure is almost certainly a reference to the fertility of the female, but the enormous, pierced ears, common to many figures of this period, have defied all theories and remain one of the great curiosities of the far past.

In the classical world, where Eros represented the unashamed delight in sexual love, most of the laughing little boys who impersonated the god were

Fertility

Above, left and right:
Father and Sons and
Mother and Daughters,
by Bartholomeus de
Bruyn the younger; gift
of Edward Drummond
Libbey, Toledo Museum
of Art, U.S.A.

Below, left: archaic
statuette of mother and
child in terra cotta;
Louvre, Paris

Above, right: Graeco-
Roman boy's head
found in a third-century
sarcophagus in Asia
Minor; Victoria and
Albert Museum

palpably portraits of known children, unlike their
descendants, the cupids of a later art, who lost all
individuality and became a mere convention.

Fertility continued to be worshipped as an ideal
for thousands of years, for in a world of famine,
pestilence and battle, with infant mortality high and
no science to the rescue, a full quiver meant hands to
till the soil and carry arms to battle. It was also an
indubitable proof of admired virility, and innumerable pictures and effigies bear witness to the honour
paid, and the losses incurred, by the prolific man
whose children, sometimes shown kneeling behind
him, each one smaller than the one before, are often
the offspring of more than one loving wife. Few
families in those days can have been as fortunate as
the German burgher and his wife seen above, he with
his five sons and she with her five daughters, all
neatly coiffed and capped.

15

THE SUBJECT of mother and child has been the most universally exploited ever since the prime symbol of Christianity became the Madonna and Child rather than the Christ Pantocrator. The anomaly of the mother worshipping her own Babe—'en effet comme c'est drôle, cet enfant qu'elle partage avec Dieu', wrote Claudel—gradually gave place to more homely pictures. Throughout the centuries every great artist repeated this theme but it was left to two women of genius, one French, one American, but both Paris-taught, to convey as no one else has been able to do the absolute essence of motherhood. Berthe Morisot and Mary Cassatt stand alone in their power to transmit the radiant and fulfilled happiness of the mother and, in the picture by Mary Cassatt above, the child's touching unawareness of the mother's intense love.

Adoration—love—and now a sense of guilty responsibility. Should one bring into this atomic age another human being destined to suffer?

Mother and Child

Left: Florentine School, National Gallery

Above: Mother and Child, Mary Cassatt

Below: Le Nouveau Né, by Bernard Buffet; permission of E. David and M. Garnier

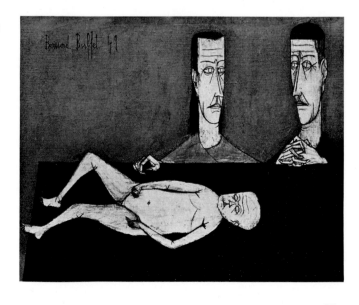

Snips 'n' Snails

THE CASUAL wear of today (*left*) is not unlike that of the early nineteenth-century boy curled up sadly in his chair below, whose long trousers, ankle-strap shoes and white socks—and wispy fringe —resemble those of his descendant.

The splendid *parures* of children in the past stated clearly their worldly status. The little Medici princess (*top right*) wearing puffed satin and jewels, like the Saxony princess beside her whose neck is encircled by as many gold chains as a grown-up's, is revealed as an important personage to be exchanged in marriage for rank or wealth.

The portrait of the little girl with the long hair (*below, right*) has an off-shoulder dress and long gloves such as the rich *bourgeoise* of her time wore. Less showy, but equally *à la mode*, is the little girl with her hair dressed high and gold ear-rings, her gown as First Empire as any her mother's can have been.

Sugar 'n' Spice

Opposite page: Boy with Toy, by Henry Lamb; National Museum of Wales. Federigo Gonzaga, by Francia; Metropolitan Museum of Art, New York. The Artist's Son, by Louis Leopold Boilly; Hallsborough Galleries

Above left: Marie de Medici, by Bronzino; Uffizi Gallery, Florence. *Right:* Princess of Saxony, by Lucas Cranach the Elder; National Gallery, Washington

Below left: Line Campineanu, by Manet; permission Wildenstein. The Artist's Daughter, by Guèrin; Museum of Boulogne-sur-Mer

The Three R's

LEARNING ONE'S lessons has always been a hard task but nowhere more so than in England. Here, the legend of the cane and the early banishment of the young still amazes the foreigner, who agrees with Osbert Sitwell that Anglo-Saxons have strange and savage customs concerned with their young. It is not much more than a century since the Fairchild Children were taken to see a murderer hanging on a gibbet as a lesson not to quarrel.

The artists who have recorded the lessons and the

learners show surprisingly little difference between the environment and the methods of different ages and places. Little boys no longer wear skirts, but they still quarrel, one cries and one denies, as they do in the fifteenth-century picture opposite.

The studious Renaissance child with a book bears a strong resemblance to Picasso's two-year-old son, and the atmosphere of the contemporary school-room continues to be unwelcoming and slightly hostile, as it has always been.

Opposite, above: detail of a predella, Ducal Palace of Urbino, by Uccello

Opposite, below: little boy reading, by Foppa; Wallace Collection

Above: portrait of the artist's two-year-old son by Picasso; Galerie Louise Leiris, Paris

Below: the Schoolroom, by Lewin Bassingthwaighte, Jeffress Gallery

DOLLS ARE nearly as old as the human race, and examples of them have been found among the remains of the oldest-known civilizations; ancient Egyptian children had wooden dolls with movable limbs, and a rag doll of the third century B.C. is still in existence. Even Ayesha, the child-bride of Mahomet, brought her dolls to her new home.

Understandably derived from the root concept of idol or image, most dolls faithfully copy the costume of their mistresses, and in the past were used extensively as ambassadors of fashion, even receiving special permits to pass between France and England when the two countries were at war.

Dolls

Opposite, left: detail from Charity, by Cranach; from the National Gallery

Opposite, right: detail from Mother and Children, by Renoir; courtesy of the Frick collection, New York

Opposite, below: Maya, daughter of the artist, with her doll, by Picasso; from the Louise Leiris Gallery, Paris

Above: Card Houses, by Chardin, Uffizi Gallery, Florence

Below: Card Houses, a portrait of his son by Antony Devas

and Guys

Just as little girls have always played with dolls, so have boys with cards, and in the game of building card-houses there is little to choose between the eighteenth century and the present day.

23

Pets

THE LOVE of children for animals has always existed, but no little boy nowadays carries a pet hawk like the one little James here wears on his wrist; nor do children own goldfinches such as are seen clutched in the hands of many small sitters in medieval pictures. Squirrels are no longer painted with their entranced owners, pet owls are rare, the golden singing canary of the last generation has been replaced by the blue budgerigar. Although dogs and cats have remained prime favourites, one breed ousts the other within a decade or two; the huge dogs which accompany the children in many eighteenth-century pictures were replaced by such small creatures as the peke and the dachshund, and now the pug, unadmired for nearly a century, has snorted its way back to favour.

Going for a ride

MOST GAMES have their origin in the principle of movement, and for their aim the discharge of superfluous energy.
One of the most popular for hundreds of years, but now alas
extinct, was the rocking-horse derived from the hobby-
horse of the Morris dancers. The favourite form of the
eighteenth and nineteenth centuries was the figure of a horse
set on a rocker (in turn replaced by swing-irons early in this
century), such as the one the little boy opposite rides with
brio, splendidly dressed in English finery and plumed hat
in spite of a tropical setting.

Pulling or riding in a cart has been a childish game ever
since the wheel was invented, and it is immaterial whether the
cart itself is beautifully made and painted scarlet, like the
one the Wedgwood children are playing with, or merely a
home-made wooden box-cart.

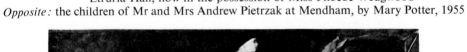

Above: the sons of Daniel Seton, Governor of the East India Company at Serat Castle, by an unknown artist, now in the possession of their descendant, Miss Seton-Kerr
Below: a detail from the painting by George Stubbs of Josiah Wedgwood and his family at Etruria Hall, now in the possession of Miss Phoebe Wedgwood
Opposite: the children of Mr and Mrs Andrew Pietrzak at Mendham, by Mary Potter, 1955

The assured well-being of the seventeenth-century children walking in a park, by Jacob Gerritsz Cuyp (Boyman's Museum, Rotterdam) contrasts poignantly with Kisling's *Frère et Sœur* (Crane Gallery, Manchester)

Brothers and Sisters

THE PAMPERED children of the rich, dressed from earliest childhood in imitation of their parents and far more precocious than our own pre-teen tots, remained a favourite subject of painting until the nineteenth century, when the romantic movement began to stress the pathos and plight of childhood. Mulready's street waifs brought tears to those Victorian eyes which remained averted from the spectacle of child-labour in the mines, and *East Lynne* was only one among many popular 'dying children' novels. With Marie Corelli's *Mighty Atom* and *Boy* the age of innocence entered into its last phase, the climate of childhood, darkened by the great shadow of education, by hitherto undreamed-of ethical and moral responsibilities, was no longer illumined by make-believe. Boys and girls are no longer the 'moving jewels' of Traherne, no longer symbols of power or romantic ideals, but rich or poor, clean or dirty, individuals in their own right.

Double drawing of a little boy's head by Tchilicheff; collection Anthony Dermey

The

Voyage Home

BY RICHARD CHURCH

1

SOONER OR later we all turn homeward. A man who dies on foreign soil is judged to have had a sad end. To escape the possibility of such a fate, every human being is possessed by an instinctive urge to hurry home. I noticed this when I was a boy, working in the laboratory in the Custom House, beside Billingsgate Market. I walked over London Bridge twice a day, morning and evening, wedged in the solid phalanx of humanity moving into London City and out of it again.

I noticed how that tide of trousered or skirted legs was sluggish in the morning, as it trickled toward offices and warehouses; how it rushed like the Severn Bore into London Bridge station after the day's work, blown by a gale of furious purpose, the desire to get home.

I felt the impulse in my own blood. What was this urge, this primitive anxiety? Are men and women infected by some racial fear of the jungle, that drives them to seek the safety of the cave, even after several thousand years of the assurances of civilization? I remember now, half a century since the routine of those years in the laboratory, more vividly than I remember all other moods and events, this eagerness to get home to my rooms on Denmark Hill. The urge often made me break into a jogtrot over London Bridge, risking my life by edging out of the crush from the pavement to the gutter. Sometimes I even had the illusion of rising above the heads of the crowd, and gliding like a seagull, levitated by my own frenzy.

It was as though I were expecting a visitor, some fabulous person, a dream-spirit, or a lover. But I knew that I should find my rooms as I had left them—empty: the breakfast cup and saucer in the sink, still to be washed; the volume of *La Fontaine's Fables* still open on the kitchen table, from which I had been memorizing those lucid phrases, to improve my knowledge of French, before setting out every morning.

I knew, too, that as I put the key in the door, and entered my solitude, a cold, sinking sensation would seize me, like a stomach cramp, as once again the cheat of anticipation worked.

Yet in spite of this consciousness, and of my reasonable efforts to control its defeatist effects, I rushed home every day breathless with anticipation. In this I was but an individual in the mortal stampede. The same intent lit the eyes and set the mouths of those thousands leaning forward as they pressed on toward the flashing Bovril advertisement at the entrance to London Bridge station yard.

Not much farther along the Borough High Street stood the Tabard Inn, from which Chaucer's Canterbury pilgrims set out six hundred years earlier. I wish he had described their home-coming. Was the expression on their faces the same as that of those twentieth-century commuters, of whom I was one?

This vestigial habit is never quite lost. Indeed, as we grow, or shrink, into old age, the craving for home revives with redoubled force, the dominant of our second childhood. It is not a matter of cowardice or timidity. People driven by the wanderlust, and those who are daredevils always out in search of adventure in 'fresh woods and pastures new', come home from time to time, to look around at the familiar scene, and to recognize it with an emotional response that is awe-stricken, mystical. Even on our travels the first thing we do on stopping for the night is to set up a simulacrum of home, temporary, but representative of and singular to our own selves; an altar to privacy.

The habit, the craving or instinct, cuts close and intimately into our lives. No outside directive, of politics, religion, or economic necessity, can wholly destroy it. A child in an orphanage will secrete a pathetic hiding place, a mouse's nest, where he may be alone with his possessions, and thus assured of that universe.

There must be some cause, outside the reach and explanations of reason, for this homing instinct. It directs the centripetal movements of all organic life. The anemone in the sea is wholly conditioned by it, and remains anchored in its own lair. The pigeon, released at the caprice of the fancier, needs only to make a few circles in the foreign air before orientating itself and winging direct for the cote.

The man who wrote of 'the kindred points of Heaven and home' was near the heart of this mystery, which controls us not only in our flight but also in our moments of rest, especially if that rest be the immobility of pain, of suffering, of despair. As we crouch away from the world, seeking like the wounded plover to merge, unobservable, into our surroundings, we contrive even to make a home of that condition. The very attributes of our person, our clothes, the contents of our pockets and bags, become aspects and symbols of home; sufficient to reassure us, if we are in mortal fear, and to preserve our sense of identity and self-respect.

Where that recognition ceases, a potentiality for crime begins. The homing instinct is the fundamental impulse toward founding a civilization, for it works upon a nomadic people, pulls them to a standstill, and thus to agriculture and the building of houses, barns, and dedicated places where thanksgiving may be offered for the fruits of these first non-destructive labours.

Having thus made human society, and the moral structures that buttress it, the home instinct at the same time reacts against its own achievement, and turns to protect the individual from the resultant tyranny of society. It gives him, and more particularly her, the impulse toward possessiveness, parental love, and the determination to hold, to shelter, his own creations. He builds the home now, not only against the elements but also against his fellow creatures. Like the other elemental passions, it works in all we do and are, both for evil and for good.

But, in speculating so generally about home, I have wandered too far from home. I intended to refer at once to an account of a recent home-coming. I see that it follows a journey so rich in contacts, sights, experiences both physical and mental, that I must come gradually to the return home. Sensation-mongers and melodramatists, people drunk on modernity and the post-war violences, will think nothing of my quiet itinerary through India and Ceylon, and of my professional pursuits there. I am not thinking of them either, for I am a sedentary person who responds slowly, perhaps belatedly, to changes, big upheavals. Home once more, and thankfully, I find myself still preparing to set out, this time in regurgitative motion, to appreciate, digest, and absorb my experiences. That will take longer than four months, the time occupied by my original journey. I foresee obstructions. Preconceived ideas and prejudices loom like rocks out of the sea and on the roads. I shall have to steer round the one, remove the other, and probably lose my bearings in the process. Memory carries a defective compass, and the caprices of the imagination are infinite, comparable to the vagaries of a kitten playing with a ball of wool. However, I am home again, and I thus have the illusion of safety, and of a fenced authority in my little world.

2

They are desperate people who cannot command one of these little worlds. Until I was recently in Calcutta I had not been able to imagine what it was like to be homeless, though my old friend, the poet W. H. Davies, had talked about it to me vividly enough. He describes in his book *The Auto-biography of a Supertramp* how he spent many years as a hobo in North America, and as a vagrant in London and the English countryside, living on his wits, a street-singer and pedlar of shoe-laces. His genius gave that life a Stevensonian glamour; but I observed that when he began to earn a little money from his writings, and was granted a Civil List pension by Mr Asquith, he gave up sleeping in doss-houses, and settled in a cottage in the village of Weald, near

Sevenoaks, lent him by Edward Thomas, a fellow poet. There he made a home, so static and peaceful a place that butterflies settled on his pencil while he sat in the garden writing verses that still enchant poetry-lovers with an ear for rhyme and a mind for lucidity.

At the beginning of this twentieth century, during the lull before the storm, the life of the vagrant was romanticized into a literary cult. Davies rode on the tide. Songs of the Open Road were fashionable, in the manner of R.L.S. and Masefield. The composers of the period set them to music heard even after the mud and blood of Flanders had dried out. But it was not popular with the unhappy warriors who came home. They had seen enough of life 'under the canopy', as Coriolanus so bitterly called it when asked where he dwelt. All they wanted was a roof overhead and a hearth of their own, before which they might accumulate the fruits of privacy, including a wife and family, thus unconsciously setting about the rebuilding of a broken civilization. But it is easier to smash than to make, and that civilization has still to be restored. Gone down with it are many of its attributes, not all of them of lasting value, or appropriate to changed needs and conditions.

The provision of homes is always a major issue. It demands priority of attention from the statesman, the priest, the economist. All three have been in despair about it, since two world wars and universal revolution have bedevilled the constructive efforts of scientist, architect, and craftsman. Subsidiary social and economic earthquakes, violent national-ism and other ideologies, not only have brought about a shortage of bricks and mortar, they have also attuned, or dis-tuned, a younger generation to an indifference to home life. How significant it is that the young Russian hero, the world's first astronaut, the idol of his countrymen and symbol of their achievement in competitive science, should be described as 'living with his wife and two children in his two-roomed flat', and that no newspapers should com-ment on this irony.

But in the domestic circumstances of the world of the mid-twentieth century Major Gagarin may be considered fortunate to have even a two-roomed flat. By comparison with millions of displaced persons, he is certainly com-fortably housed. I try to appreciate his content of mind, and even that of his wife, by recalling what I saw in Calcutta, a city of 5,000,000 souls. I call them souls, to remind myself that 30,000 of them are capable of that attribute, though driven from East Pakistan to squat on the pavements of Calcutta, waiting for something to be done for them.

They are to be seen in the very heart of the city, lying asleep, or dying, beneath filthy rags on the traffic islands, while the noonday flood of cars and lorries roars round them. There they lie, inert, immobile. Nobody even lifts the rag from a hidden face to find out if this be sleep or death.

Religion does not solve this problem. The Indian people are spiritual in a way that Europeans are not. Every moment of their lives, every gesture, habit, and reaction to circumstance, are conditioned by this consciousness which occupies the forefront of their minds: the dominance and superior importance of the spiritual matters over the material concerns of everyday life. That may be why they accept physical suffering, other people's and their own, as of minor importance. Their indifference to this degradation of the homeless and hungry millions is terrifying to an observer from a modern Welfare State.

The Vice-President of India, Dr Radhakrishnan, a philosopher-statesman of noble character, said to me that this problem of 'poverty and population' was the principal anxiety of the Government. But I thought that the people in general were not thus concerned. They were not ashamed, nor desperate about it. They walked past these half-human derelicts, on their way to the temples of Siva, Krishna, or Buddha, wrapped in a sincere religious fervour of a kind found only in the few zealots among Western communities.

How can these conditions be reconciled by a rational observer? I saw the contrast even more shockingly presented up-country, at Budd-gaya, the place where Buddha is supposed to have sat under a tree and to have received Enlightenment. There stands the tree, not gigantic and not a banyan, backed by a garish altar. Behind them towers the *stupa* or temple, overloaded with ornament and symbolical carving. It denies and reverses the principles and practice of the Buddha, just as the florid temples over the tomb of St Francis of Assisi deny his vow of poverty and the whole purpose of his mission.

Squatting round the *stupa* lay groups of Tibetan refugees. They were even more filthy and degraded than the refugees in Calcutta. In spite of the heat on that plain of Bihar, they wore their mat-like native garments and moccasins. The clothes clung to them rather as the protective accretions cling to a caddis-worm. The stench polluted even the holy air of the garden surrounding the temple. They sat delousing one another, until we appeared. Then they rushed at us, whining and crying, clawing at the car window. One old crone had dead eyes and a drooling mouth. She kept up a feeble moan, scratching at the windscreen with her nails. The children pushed her aside, to swarm round us as we walked to the temple, but she reappeared when we returned. Her claws were hardly larger than those of the begging children, who by now were screaming at us in a kind of mock fury.

In moods of despair, when we look out at this world menace of 'poverty and population', and at the hostility of totalitarian governments to the privacy and dignity of the individual, we may wonder if the human race has had its day and is now rushing to the brink. Will the end come soon, in a hydrogen holocaust, or shall mankind gradually crush itself under the pressure of population? Hitherto, we have never made weapons without using them. Either from prejudice or stupidity, the majority of people will not practise birth-control. So human life must either be exterminated soon or degraded later.

Such cynical, fatalistic thoughts are too general to interest us for long. The particular event, here and now, offers more drama, though miniature. That is because it is personal, part of the individual's home-coming. What then is this controlling passion that takes command as soon as consciousness dawns in the child's mind and remains insistent throughout life, undeflected by the multitude of other desires and impulses that drag us aside on the journey? Even those mortals who are indifferent to a lodging on this earth, wanderers and Ishmaels who cannot find or accept a shelter, within yet isolated from the community, are nevertheless driven on by this craving for 'a fine and private place', though their only domestication will be in the grave, their only settled property the 'entail of four planks'.

Certainly I was mastered by that craving, days before
the moment came when I boarded the *Oriana* at Colombo.
My wife and I had been on the move for four months,
latter-day wandering scholars, each with our offerings. I
talked, and gave readings, at the universities. She, being a
silversmith and jeweller, sought out the craftsmen who in
India still work by hand at little benches shaped exactly
like her own, which stands on a balcony in our living-room
at home. This coincidence alone would have given her
confidence, had she not discovered also that the Indian tools,
and the handling of them, were familiar.

Our travels therefore had not been without interest.
We had quartered the sub-continent, with the exception
of Pakistan; met hundreds of hospitable people, from the
Prime Minister and Vice-President down to the cleaner and
sweeper (formerly called the Untouchables); visited temples
and sculptured caverns; driven over semi-deserts and through
the jungle; sweated in aquarian Trivandrum and shivered in
Chandigahr. I had talked publicly until I was voiceless,
and my wife had filled her pocket sketch-book with formal
designs. But now, engulfing all this excitement and experience, rose the longing to return home. It had begun to
show itself during a bout of tropical sickness three weeks
earlier when we reached Ceylon. During our last few days
in Colombo it became almost uncontrollable, and I gave my
two final lectures at the Buddhist University almost in a
condition of self-hypnotism, combating this craving.

I spoke to an audience of several hundred monks and
young seminarists, and a scattering of picturesque folk
invited by the Principal. The sun was going down after a
hot day. His beams shone through the large, open audi-
torium, and threw horizontal shadows from the pillars
supporting this ornate pavilion. They lay across the crowded
floor, so deep in contrast to the livid fire of the sunset that
the people sitting in those shadows were almost extinguished,
while those in sunlight burned like lamps, their saffron
robes, their eyeballs, their shaven craniums, each bare
shoulder and arm flashing as though moulded in metal.

To add to the conflagration a News Film unit trained
its lights and cameras at the high rostrum where I sat beside

the chairman, the Professor of Philosophy, a figure not unlike Pope John; very Roman, very severe, very formal. After some prayers and responses, a Buddhist litany in Sinhalese, I was introduced and began to talk, to the twirl of the cameras and the obbligato of voices and noises-off which combine with all lecturing in the Orient.

Speaking in public in any place outside Europe is exhausting work, because the lecturer is never alone with his audience. He has to collect and unify its attention in an environment of open doors and windows, a constant coming and going of cultural camp-followers, the rivalry of loud conversation, children at play, traffic blocks, sudden hysterias of political demonstrations, against the shout-throw of the lecture-room. In addition, there is the ceaseless hoicking of the hordes of crows, those scavengers of the East, who perch on the window-ledges and croak their disapproval of all that is being said from the dais.

The speaker has no need to be disconcerted, or to fear that he will never weld his listeners into a mass-personality (that desideratum of the orator). Indian audiences, once their attention is caught, are deaf to extraneous attraction. They lean forward, their eyes intent, their brows corrugated under the pressure of seeming interest, quite unaware that the lecturer, if he is a pampered European, is suffering acutely from the effort to ignore the bursts of *joie de vivre* from the corridors, and the hubbub from the streets. This is indeed an obbligato, and not merely an accompaniment, for it claims equality with the solo of the speaker.

During these two last lectures in Colombo I shared my audience's imperviousness. But I was also distracted from my own voice, even from my own thoughts, under the compulsion of this desire that by now was dominant over mind and body. My limbs ached with the longing for home, and as I stood on that rostrum, high above my shadow-striped audience, massive as rock below me, I found my consciousness splitting into halves, the one still dealing with the subject of my talk, still holding my audience together, while the other was carrying me out along one of those solid sunbeams, past the white *stupa* shining in the courtyard beyond, out to the harbour, and the ship reported to be steaming up toward Ceylon from Australia, on its way to pick me up and to carry me to my home.

This is not a matter easily to be dramatized and put to literary account. Like the authority of sleep, it claims everybody, from birth to death, and expresses itself only through other states of mind: fear, loneliness, maybe even cowardice, prejudice, and ignorance. Can an emotion which employs such communicants be a worthy one? Is the home, the family enclosure, a relic of the childhood of civilization, when mankind's environment was always dangerous, an unexplored jungle? Communist peoples may see it that way, and thus find a reason for suppressing family life and the home which is its centre.

But what is to replace it, and its infinite attributes, whose influence penetrates into a person's consciousness with a complex subtlety comparable to the minute veins and nerve-threads that co-ordinate and control his body? I cannot conceive how a man would think, feel, act, who has no basis of home-craving. But, as populations grow tumid, some kind of mass control will intervene, a totalitarian system that must override the individual and his privacy, we shall rear vast communities that may have no experience and no conception of home-life. Will they still be human, as we know the humanity hitherto moulded by civilization? Will privacy be possible, or desired?

These questions, surely, weigh down our minds with dread, though maybe already generations are growing up to whom our fears are incomprehensible. They are already conditioned, and would dismiss my speculation as reactionary, sentimental, a by-blow of the superstitions of 'religion'.

The fox is a home-lover without being prompted by religion. Even the ant and bee, wholly reared in communistic societies, have this prejudice in favour of their own queen-mother, symbol of home. No political surgery will root out this urge from the blood-stream. I can write of it with an unshakable faith in its permanence, and its future influence on the conduct, habits, beliefs, and hopes of individual men and women. It will therefore continue to emerge, especially in times and circumstances of crisis, as a force in the community of mankind, even when politics have been dissolved in a world federation and there are no more nations, if such an outcome be possible.

A Symposium of STYLES

Art Nouveau

BY BARBARA MORRIS

L'ART NOUVEAU, described by Walter Crane as 'that strange decorative disease', arose through the desire of artists and craftsmen to free themselves from the fetters of past convention. *L'Art Nouveau,* a movement rather than a mere decorative style, reached a brilliant flowering at the turn of the nineteenth century, to die out within a decade through its own excesses. Few movements have in their own day excited so much heated discussion and such violently opposed views. On the one hand, *l'Art Nouveau* was regarded as the 'hope of life', on the other as 'the outcome of degeneracy'. Today, some sixty years later, we can see the movement in perspective and appreciate the beauty and originality of its finest expressions.

In different countries it flourished under different names. In France it was for a time known as the *style nouille* or even

A page from Aubrey Beardsley's MORTE D'ARTHUR

the *style de bouche de Métro*; in Belgium as *la Libre Esthét-ique* or *le Style des Vingt*; in Germany as the *Jugendstil* or the derogatory *Bandwurmstil* (tape-worm style); while in Italy it was known as the *stile Inglese* or *stile Liberty*, after the well-known London store, but finally *l'Art Nouveau* was accepted internationally as an all-embracing term.

It is difficult to sum up the characteristics of *l'Art Nouveau* in precise terms, but the main features are an unusual emphasis upon the ornamental value of the line—an undulating, flowing, flaming line—combined with an extraordinary synthesis of ornament and form, so that the ornament seems to fuse with the structure. Pale, languid colours were preferred; soft greys, milky whites, subdued pinks and lilac, olive and sage greens—the green of the stems and leaves of succulent plants, touched by an opalescent sheen. For inspiration *l'Art Nouveau* turned to nature, but to nature in its more unexpected forms—the bottom of the sea, the undulating seaweed, the octopus with its writhing tentacles, even the waves of the sea itself. The *art nouveau* artist sought inspiration in the more exotic plants, the pale exotic plants of the hot-house and lily pond, rather than the simple wild flowers of field and hedgerow. He was obsessed by the stem, elongating and twisting it and fascinated by the tendrils of the vine rather than the plant itself. The bud was often more interesting than the full-blown blossom.

When *l'Art Nouveau* was concerned with the human form there was a preoccupation with the female figure almost to the exclusion of the male. The most fascinating aspect of all was the hair, described by a contemporary writer as 'a wealth of whirling, flowing, human hair. . . . Loosen the formal restrained classic coil from its rigid fixedness and let the breeze play with it; or borrow a long curling lock from a Botticelli painting or travel even further, and steal out of a Japanese picture the blue winding dragon line . . . a line of subtle, undulating beauty, a movement of vibrating life.'

L'Art Nouveau claimed to be the new art of the new time; yet its break with tradition was never quite complete and elements of past styles are inherent in it. In France, at least, it to some extent merged with the rococo revival of the late nineteenth century and the asymmetrical ornamentation and vigorous curves, derived from the baroque and rococo, are essential features of *art nouveau*. The interlaced ornament, coiled spirals, and strange beasts of Celtic art also find their place in *l'Art Nouveau*; especially in the work of Charles Rennie Mackintosh and the Glasgow School. The ornament of late Gothic architectural detail, the Curvilinear in England and the Flamboyant in France, with its flamelike tracery, flowing detail, and double-curved ogee arches, also plays its part. The art of Japan, rediscovered in the 1860s, was another important source of inspiration. Japanese bronzes, with natural plants fusing with the form of the vessel,

undoubtedly influenced the *art nouveau* silversmiths and metal-workers, but it was probably the Japanese print that made the greatest impact.

The influence of the Japanese print is most clearly seen in the work of Aubrey Beardsley, whose book illustrations set the pattern for the Continental *art nouveau* periodicals, particularly the German *Pan*. Taking as his starting point the pages of William Morris's Kelmscott books, in 1893 Beardsley produced an outstanding edition of Malory's *Morte d'Arthur*, providing a remarkable synthesis of the Japanese with the languid Pre-Raphaelite figures of Burne-Jones and Rossetti. The result was something that was wholly *art nouveau.* The subtle relationship of black and white, the brilliant patterning, and the perfect balance of the asymmetrical composition derive clearly from the Japanese print. The strange exotic plants, with their long flowing stems and undulating movement, were to set the pattern for many textiles and wallpapers in the decade to follow.

There is little doubt that Beardsley forms one of the links between *l'Art Nouveau* and the Pre-Raphaelites. Although the English tended to regard *l'Art Nouveau* as primarily a Continental movement, even at the time a number of authorities recognized that its roots in fact lay in England. Siegfried Bing, whose *Maison de l'Art Nouveau*, established in Paris in 1895, gave the name to the movement, stated that 'the initial movement began in England, under the influence of the Pre-Raphaelites and the ideas of Ruskin, and was carried into practical affairs by the admirable genius of William Morris'. In similar vein, Hermann Muthesius, the German architect, wrote that 'the example of England set off the new movement. The whole world turned in a new direction; England had shown to art the way into a new country.'

Ruskin and Morris provided no direct inspiration for *l'Art Nouveau* but their ideas paved the way for a new flowering of design. In the work of the architect and designer A. H. Mackmurdo, however, we find *l'Art Nouveau* in its full maturity more than a decade before it was to become a recognized style. Mackmurdo became a friend of William Morris in 1880 and many of his designs show the influence of Morris, but his title page for *Wren's City Churches* displays a complete break with established conventions. Here in this design of 1883, which echoes a design for a chair produced two years earlier, Mackmurdo presents all the essential features of *l'Art Nouveau*. Here are the sinuous curves with the leaves and petals undulating like tongues of flame. The same swaying rhythm is even more marked in his printed textile, the 'Cromer Bird'. Over a lightly patterned background, tufts of seaweed float from left to right, accompanied by swift flying birds, counterbalanced by strange disembodied plants streaming in the opposite direction. The same flowing movement can be seen in the textiles and wallpapers designed by Walter Crane and C. F. A. Voysey, and indeed it was in the field of flat pattern that the English made the most important contribution to *l'Art Nouveau*.

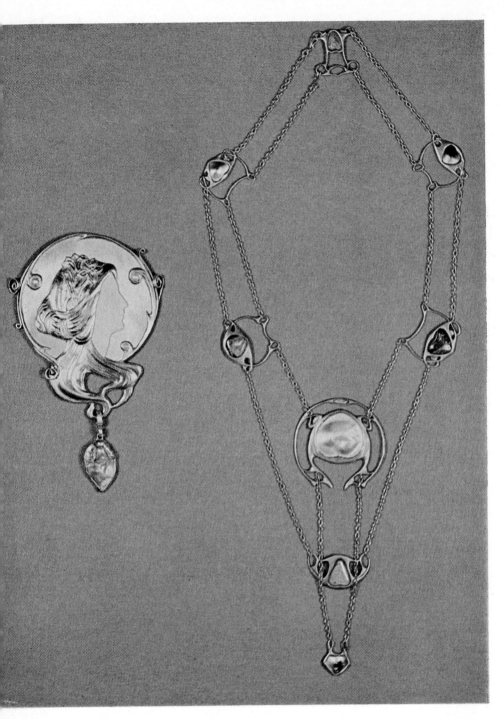

THE pendant, of mother-of-pearl, ivory, and silver parcel gilt, was made by the English jeweller A. C. C. Jahn at the beginning of this century and shows the influence of French *art nouveau*. The gold necklet, set with opals and mother-of-pearl, was made by the Birmingham firm of Haseler about 1903 for the 'Cymric' range of Liberty jewellery. Both pieces are in the Victoria and Albert Museum.

THIS cloth book binding, with gilt decoration, was designed by Aubrey Beardsley (1872–98) for his illustrated edition of Thomas Malory's *Morte d'Arthur*, published in 1893. The flowing grace of his line is captured in the sinuous stems and leaves of the exotic plants and the motif is echoed in the line decorations in the text. Beardsley's work had a profound influence on the work of the Glasgow School and a remarkable series of *art nouveau* bindings were produced by Talwin Morris (1865–1911) about the turn of the century. Talwin Morris, who also designed furniture, metalwork, and stained glass, was a leading exponent of the Glasgow style. He became art director of Blackie and Sons in 1890, and most of their outstanding bindings were from his hand.

THE 'Cromer Bird' textile was designed by A. H. Mackmurdo for the Century Guild and printed in shades of gold and reddish brown by Simpson and Godlee in 1884. Mackmurdo preferred a warm palette and many of his fabrics were printed in reds and orange, which seemed to emphasize the flame-like quality of his designs. Some of Mackmurdo's patterns show the influence of William Morris—indeed, even in this design there is a hint of Morris in the use of a subsidiary pattern in the background—but the strong sense of movement is entirely Mackmurdo's own and presents a remarkable anticipation of full-fledged *art nouveau* a decade before the style had emerged as a recognized fashion.

IN England *art nouveau* was perhaps more apparent in the design of textiles and wallpapers than in any other field. By 1900 most firms were producing *art nouveau* designs even in the cheapest ranges. The textile above, with mauve poppies on a deep green ground, was printed by F. Steiner & Co. in 1903. The fabric on the right, printed in shades of blue, was designed by Harry Napper (*d.* 1930) for Turnbull and Stockdale in 1903. Napper was more successful than any other English designer in absorbing the spirit of Continental *nouveau*. He was responsible for some of the most striking *art nouveau* designs recently revived by Libertys.

THE architect C. F. A. Voysey (1857–1941) designed his first textiles and wallpapers in 1883 under the direct influence of Mackmurdo. The original design (*below*) was made in 1889 and is wholly *art nouveau* in spirit. Designs such as this had a marked influence on the Continent, for Voysey's work was much admired and illustrated abroad. Voysey himself stated that he thought 'the condition which has made *l'Art Nouveau* possible is a distinctly healthy development, but at the same time the manifestation of it is distinctly unhealthy and revolting. . . . Conceit and apish imitation seem to be the chief features.'

IN spite of his views, many of Voysey's designs were pure *art nouveau*. The silk and wool double-cloth (*above*) designed for Alexander Morton and Co. of Carlisle in 1898 is a wholly characteristic example with its flat, twisting leaves and swiftly flying birds. The introduction of birds into the design became almost a hallmark of Voysey's style, and, like William Morris, he turned directly to nature for inspiration, although his forms were undoubtedly more conventionalized. Another prolific designer of wallpapers was Walter Crane (1845–1915) whose 'Day Lily' wallpaper, printed by Jeffrey and Co. in 1897, is illustrated in colour on page 60.

THE distinctive and extraordinary manner of decoration that became known throughout Europe as the 'Glasgow Style' evolved in the 1890s at the Glasgow School of Art. Charles Rennie Mackintosh (1868–1928), who entered the school in 1885, was to become the leading exponent of the Glasgow style, working in close collaboration with his wife, Margaret Macdonald, her sister Frances, and his friend Herbert McNair. Their co-operation was so close, and the affinity of their individual works so

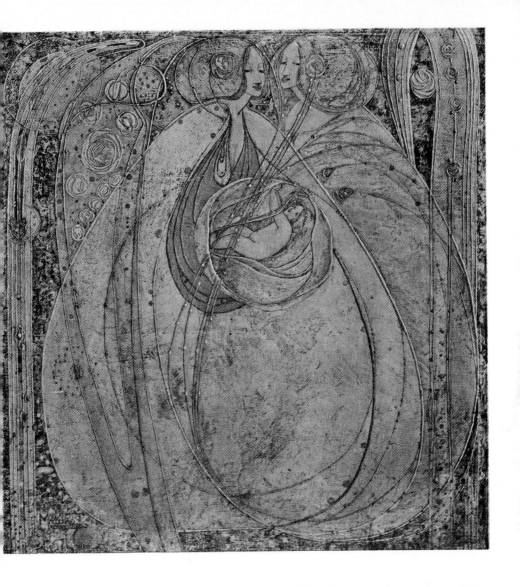

marked, that they became known as 'the Four'. The beaten copper plaques (*opposite, left*), belonging to Dr Thomas Howarth, were made by the two sisters in 1896, and the sconce (*opposite, right*) was made by them in 1896 and is now at the Glasgow School of Art. The strange weird figures seem creatures from a dream world while the intricate linear design seems to derive from Celtic art. The soft pearly colours of the gesso panel (*above*) were beloved by the Four. This panel was executed by Margaret Macdonald for Mackintosh's 'Rose Boudoir' at the Turin Exhibition of 1902.

The silver dish and spoon (*opposite*), belonging to Mrs Shirley Bury, were designed by C. R. Ashbee (1863–1942), the founder and chief designer of the Guild of Handicraft. The work of the Guild was well known and admired abroad about the turn of the century, particularly in Germany and Austria.

THE silver brooch (*right*) was designed by Margaret and Frances Macdonald for Jessie R. Newbery, the wife of the principal of Glasgow School of Art, in 1895, and is now in the possession of her daughter, Mrs Mary Sturrock. Jessie R. Newbery taught embroidery at the school from 1894 to 1908. The cushion cover (*below*), worked in crewel wools and now in the Victoria and Albert Museum, was designed by her in 1899.

The silver gilt badge and chain (*opposite*), belonging to the Royal Institute of Painters in Watercolours, were designed by Sir Alfred Gilbert (1854–1934) about 1891 and show a remarkable anticipation of later *art nouveau*. Although Gilbert himself abhorred the style—'*L'Art Nouveau* forsooth! Absolute nonsense!'—and dismissed the productions of the movement as 'vapid, disloyal, unhealthy', there seems little doubt that his work had a significant influence particularly on French *art nouveau* jewellers.

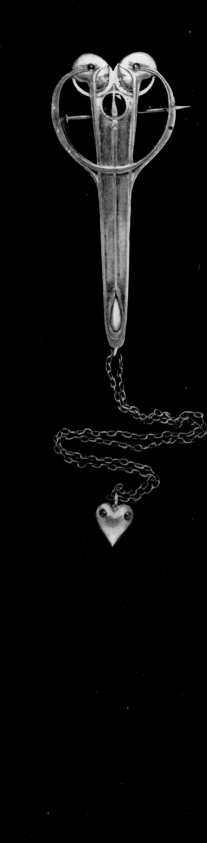

53

FRENCH *art nouveau* centred round Geoffrey Bing's '*L'Art Nouveau*' in Paris, and the town of Nancy, where the architectural setting of the city, with its rococo façades and gilded ironwork, provided a stimulating background for the development of the new design. The two trays (*opposite*) designed by Emile Gallé (1846–1904) and Louis Majorelle (1859–1926) show the skilful use of marquetry which was to distinguish the work of the *art nouveau* furniture designers of the Nancy school. Gallé was inspired by the local flora of his native Lorraine, translating the wildflowers of the lowland and forest into living designs, and the free asymmetry of the Morning Glory on his tray (*above, opposite*) are characteristic of his style. Majorelle's tray (*below*) shows the influence of Japanese art. Majorelle first designed in the neo-rococo style but adopted *art nouveau* in 1897–8 under the influence of Gallé.

The three textiles (*right*) were printed by the Lancashire firm of F. Steiner & Co. The poppy design (*centre*), dating from 1900, has the free-flowing naturalism that is found in Gallé's work, but the other two designs, dating from 1903, show the more angular stylization that was to characterize *art nouveau* designs after the turn of the century.

THE tall cabinet of wood (*left*), stained purple, veneered with kingwood, and enriched with marquetry and mounts of wrought iron, was designed by Louis Majorelle and shown in Paris in 1900. Majorelle's work has a marked plastic quality and the braces and structural elements of his furniture become shoots and branches. This cabinet forms part of a large group of continental *art nouveau* furniture purchased from the Paris Exhibition of 1900 by George Donaldson, one of the jurors, for presentation to the Victoria and Albert Museum. The exhibition of this furniture at the Museum in the spring of 1901 brought forth a storm of controversy, so outrageous did it seem to conservative tastes. Some people, however, recognized that here was something important and something that would provide a stimulus to English design, and that here was an art that had something new to say. In the words of Alexandre Charpentier: 'This will create new and unsuspected relationships between forms; in fact, it will create new forms, new lines, and new harmonies . . . it will exist upon living symbols.'

THE three pieces shown here are the work of English silversmiths. The pewter butter-dish and knife, belonging to Mrs Shirley Bury, were designed about 1903 for the Liberty range of 'Tudric' pewter. The silver casket, now in the Victoria and Albert Museum, was made by William Hutton & Sons and bears the London hallmark for 1902–3. The silver tray, belonging to Mrs Shirley Bury, registered in 1901, shows the influence of Continental *art nouveau* on the Birmingham silversmiths at the turn of the century.

EMILE GALLÉ received practical experience of the art of glass-making in his father's workshops and in the Meisenthal glass factory in the Saar Valley. During a stay in England he studied the overlay glass technique of the Chinese and Japanese snuff-bottles at the Victoria and Albert Museum. In this vase (*left*), purchased by that Museum in 1900, the poetic quality of Gallé's work is ably demonstrated. The various layers have been cut away to form the relief decoration and the flowing plant forms fuse with the shape.

similar organic quality is shown in the dish of clear glass (*above*), decorated with an applied silver leaf ground and green glass trailings. It was made at the Brierley Hill glassworks of Stevens and Williams about 1900 and is now in the possession of John Northwood, Esq.

RENÉ JULES LALIQUE (1860–1945) was undoubtedly the greatest French jeweller of the *art nouveau* period. He was not only a brilliant designer but a technical innovator of great importance and made use of precious and semi-precious stones, gold in many shades, opaque and translucent enamel, and modest materials such as horn, combining these materials in a new and original manner. The comb of carved horn (*top left*), enriched with rose diamonds, gold, and enamel, was made about 1903. The snakes (*top right*) of enamelled silver gilt, shown at the Paris Exhibition of 1900, and the corsage ornament (*below*) of gold openwork set with diamonds, opals, and enamel, were both made in 1898. The three pieces belong to the Gulbenkian Foundation and are superb examples of Lalique's fertile imagination and mastery of technique.

In England *l'Art Nouveau* was always tempered by restraint, and the English designers rarely perpetrated the excesses of some of the Continental exponents of the style. In their desire to free themselves of all conventions some of the designers tended to ignore the basic qualities of the materials with which they worked. In the words of one contemporary writer 'all respect for materials has been cast to the winds. Wood is cut as though it were a grainless and fibreless structure like cheese; metal is twisted into the most weird and wonderful shapes, chairs appear as clumps of gnarled tree roots, twisted boughs conspire to form a bedstead . . . walls show trees with their roots in the skirting boards and foliage in the ceiling. Nowhere is the purpose of an article honourably expressed. The electric lights must masquerade in pools under the eyes of a nymph . . . snakes twisted into ingenious knots for stair balusters threaten you as you ascend, the door knocker becomes a grinning satyr and even the carpet casts malevolent eyes at you as you traverse it.'

Excesses such as these, and the readiness with which its characteristic forms seemed to lend themselves to cheap commercial exploitation, signalled the end of *l'Art Nouveau* as a vital force. *L'Art Nouveau* had reached its climax at the Paris Exhibition of 1900. In commercial productions, in wallpapers, textiles, pewter, silver, and pottery, it lingered on for another decade, surviving even until the First World War, but as far as the *avant-garde* designers were concerned, the International Exhibition at Turin in 1902 saw its final flowering. Walter Crane, in 1903, stated that his impression was that 'what is generally understood by *l'Art Nouveau* is already *old*. Its apotheosis was at Turin last year . . . the new art carried seeds of dissolution in itself.'

Those who had led the movement began to abandon the sinuous curves for right-angled bends; the geometrical forms of the square, the rhomboid, the circle, and the oval were preferred to the organic forms of the stalk and leaf, the wave and the flowing hair. But *l'Art Nouveau* had fulfilled its function; it had shaken off the dead hand of the eclectic historicism of the nineteenth century and freed the designer from the dry formulae of the ornamental grammars.

E

SOUTH AFRICAN ROCOCO

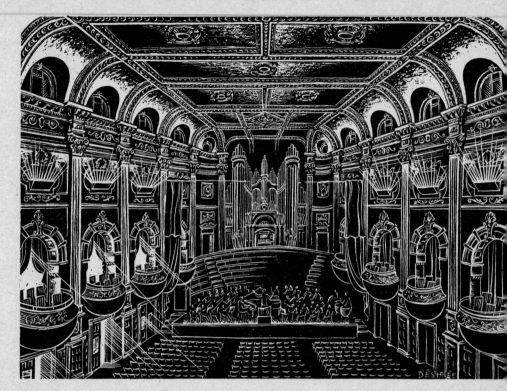

Written & Illustrated by Desirée Picton-Seymou

AT THE height of the 'cast-iron' era gold and diamonds were discovered in southern Africa. The older cities expanded, new towns sprang up in the middle of nowhere —in 1885 Johannesburg was still farm land in the Transvaal Republic, with Paul Krüger as President and Pretoria as the rather rural capital. The Orange Free State was a separate republic and Natal and the Cape Colony were outposts of British Empire.

Lacy cast-iron verandahs—*stoeps*—are well suited to the South African climate of extreme heat and violent rain, and throughout the country there can be found infinite variations on the use of the 'pre-fab' sections of ironwork, from small country cottages with just a verandah (usually hung with ferns and aspidistras) to the early office blocks of the mining towns, to say nothing of a good selection of memorials, lamp standards, park benches, fountains, and bandstands.

Above is Grand Hall, the City Hall in Cape Town—ornate with dusty plaster-work and interchangeable with any other British provincial town hall of the 1900s. The approach to the Grand Hall is up 'corned-beef' marble steps, past modestly draped white marble ladies and *art-nouveau* stained-glass windows. On royal occasions the chandeliers spout ostrich feathers. But the chief function of the Hall is a home for the Municipal Orchestra.

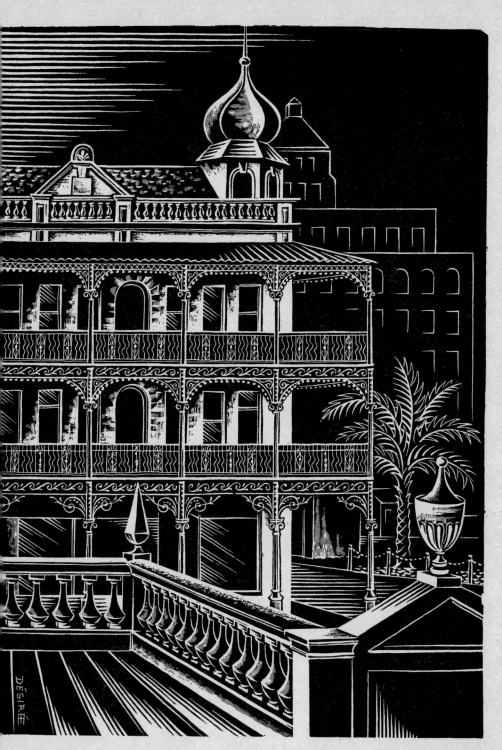

THE BUILDING across the way and of slightly earlier date is a charming example of many-storeyed cast-iron balconies; the onion dome over the corner of the roof is repeated higher up this long street on minarets of Cape Town's Malay quarter.

DÉSIRÉE

WITH THE temperature as hot outside as inside, this conservatory in St. George's Park, Port Elizabeth, houses tropical greenery and a gorgeous collection of orchids, also a decorative selection of ironwork. The exterior is elegantly bulbous, with cast-iron 'crestings' of honeysuckle design. The surrounding park is peculiarly English and at all times seems to be deserted—there is a strange and eerie memorial to the Boer War, a vast balustraded arena in the centre of which is a pond, now dry, and from this rises a cast-iron edifice with lions, pillars, and every possible decoration. On top stands a soldier of the period with fixed bayonet.

IF YOU 'struck lucky' with gold, diamonds, or ostrich feathers, this was your dream house, Palm Villa, Jacob Marè Street, Pretoria. A few doors away is the equally pretentious Melrose House, occupied by Lord Roberts when the Treaty of Vereeniging was signed at the termination of the Boer War.

IN 1497 Vasco da Gama, bound for India, sailed round the Cape of Good Hope in the *San Rafael*. The African coast, where he landed on Christmas Day, he named Natal in honour of the Nativity. To honour Vasco da Gama, the Victorians erected this cast-iron edifice in the midst of Durban Docks, entirely concocted from parts illustrated in the delicately steel-engraved catalogues of the foundries. Every inch is decorated, and from under the dome cast-iron owls stare at you.

66

WITH FOLLIES and turrets, ornate with plaster-work, balconies of iron, and sweeping steps and terraces, the Durban Club looks out upon coconut palms, heavy scented frangi-pangi, and a sea of tropical blue. Inside is much green leather and mahogany, very reminiscent of its London counterparts.

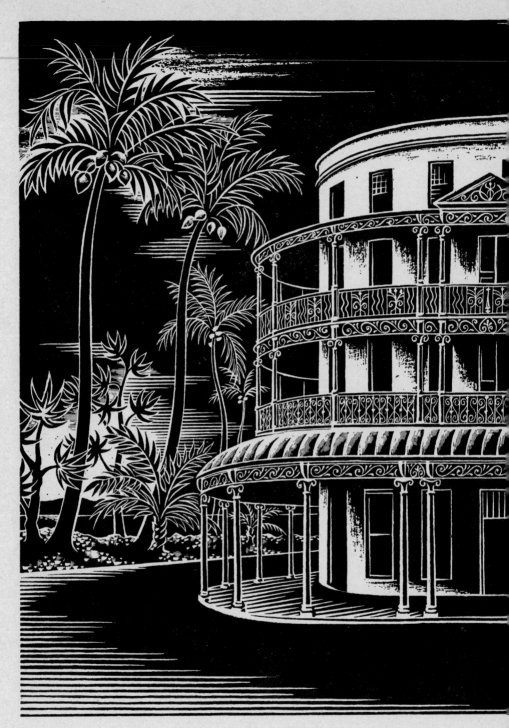

NEAR THE Durban Club and facing the Esplanade is Twine's Hotel, threaten
with demolition, and one of the prettiest buildings of its era, combining Georg
simplicity with tropical lacework. The building which curves round the oppo

rner is solid but graceful; both are well suited to the intense and humid heat.

ese hotels, with their high-ceilinged spaciousness, are reminiscent of more

surely days.

STRETCHING FROM the Docks to the lower slopes of Table Mountain, Long Street has a charm peculiar to Cape Town. Whole blocks of buildings still remain with double-storeyed Victorian iron *stoeps*, varied in design and painted every imaginable colour. Some of the buildings are equally exuberant, surmounted by obelisks and urns, while others are flat-faced Georgian buildings 'modernized' in the 1890s. In this street, too, are many-storeyed modern office blocks interspersed with mosques and churches of various denominations.

UNFORTUNATELY, THE arcade opposite, between Market and Commissioner Streets in Johannesburg, has now had its roof removed; but once it had pride of place as an example in the catalogue of the foundry (Walter MacFarlane of Glasgow) that designed it. A Johannesburg guide of 1893 quotes—'a favourite resort for ladies, who, when shopping, have been driven to seek shelter from the dust and rain'.

70

71

COMPLETELY VICTORIAN and unchanged throughout seventy-five years—except for the chandeliers being converted from gas to electricity—the Queen's Hall in the Houses of Parliament, Cape Town, leaves nothing to the imagination. Everywhere is decoration; the floor is tiled, the columns green marble, the doors with elaborate sand-blasted glass panels; the mahogany gallery railing is of strange design. The plaster-work and ceiling are all ornate, and the whole is given a strange subterranean atmosphere by the amber glass in the windows.

APPROACHED FROM street level through an elaborate iron gate and up a flight of marble steps the 'vestibule' of the Exploration Buildings in Johannesburg (opposite) is definitely a surprise. Built in a 'pre-fab' manner, this triumph of ironwork dates from 1894, and was supplied by the St Pancras Ironwork Co. Ltd of London. The floors are of glass blocks set into an iron framework, and the lift is an elaborate iron cage. The plaster-work is in the 'Renaissance Manner', likewise the vast sandstone exterior.

72

LOOKING MORE like a casino, seen across lawns and sub-tropical greenery and past a disapproving Queen Victoria, the Houses of Parliament in Cape Town were once considered 'the most handsome buildings in the Colony'. Erected in 1886 at a cost of £220,000, the site was at the lower end of what was in the seventeenth century Jan van Riebeeck's vegetable garden for the Dutch East India Company.

AT THE top of Alphen Hill, looking across False Bay to the Indian Ocean on one side and across Wynberg Camp Parade Ground to Table Mountain on the other, 'Salubritas' was built towards the end of last century for a mayor of Wynberg (today Wynberg comes under Cape Town Municipality). Great care was taken in choosing this wonderful site, and great care too must have gone into the building of this 'wedding cake'. The garden was laid out in a romantic manner with terraces and urns, palm trees and camellias, and sweet-scented 'moon-flowers', and always the cool trickle of the water from a lichen-covered carved granite fountain.

Left: Methodist Church, Johannesburg. *Top and bottom:* Groote Kerk, Pretoria
Right: Paul Krüger Kerk, Pretoria

76

American Gothic

BY JOHN MAASS

GRANT WOOD won immediate fame when his 'American Gothic' was exhibited in 1930. Though intended as satire, the painting (in the Art Institute of Chicago) was hailed as a patriotic masterpiece; the title has become part of the language.

GOTHIC WAS doubly enchanting to Americans of the Romantic era because it was not only long ago but far away. America lacked the Romantics' favourite specimens of 'pleasing decay'; there were no ancient cathedrals, no ruined castles, no broken abbeys. The Gothic Revival came to America with rare suddenness—quite unlike the gradual advent of its English parent. In 1834 William Ross, an English visitor to New York, could still write: 'The Greek mania here is at its height, as you infer from the fact that everything is a Greek temple from the privies in the back court through the various grades of prison, theatre, church, custom-house, and state-house.' Within a decade the Greeks were on the wane and the Goths triumphant. The same Americans who had proclaimed Grecian and Roman buildings as uniquely appropriate to a republic convinced themselves with complete sincerity that these heathen styles were objectionable in a Christian country.

The Victorians knew that architecture is essentially a symbolic art, and they worked hard—sometimes too hard—to make every building a 'fitting' symbol. The aesthetes' doctrines of *l'art pour l'art* and 'significant form' were yet unborn; the Gothic Revival gloried in its sentimental content and literary associations. The English-born architect Gervase Wheeler wrote in 1851: 'We of the Saxon race feel somehow always a home-whispering voice at the heart when we gaze upon some crumbling beauty in our nation's birthplace across the ocean. The growing fondness for "Gothic Cottages" seems to show that the inborn feeling is seeking outer vent.' Andrew Jackson Downing, the popular writer on building and gardening, praised the 'Old English' villa style which would call to mind 'the hearty hospitality, the joyous old sports, the romance and chivalry, which invest it with a kind of golden glow'.

Gothic Revival design shared the American scene with the Italianate and French modes; there was no 'battle of styles' but peaceful co-existence. American Gothic was a part of the nineteenth century's very own style of Picturesque Eclecticism. The emphasis is on 'picturesque'. The structure of Gothic architecture was still a sealed book; only its outward image was glimpsed through romantic engravings and lithographs. Any close copying was an impossibility in a country where formally trained architects could be counted on the fingers of two hands. American Gothic was the pleasant fruit of ignorance.

In the last quarter of the nineteenth century architectural colleges were established, American students went to the École des Beaux Arts, measured drawings and photographs appeared. Thousands of Neo-Gothic churches and schools of deadly correctness are the stony results of this increased knowledge. Julien Guadet was right when he wrote in 1902: 'Archaeology, which should be the handmaiden of the arts, can become their most formidable enemy.'

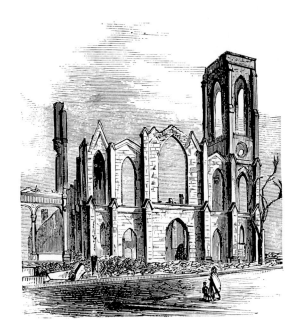

Opposite: Netley Abbey in Hampshire—'Yon parted roofs that nod aloft in Air, The threat'ning Battlement, the rifted Tow'r . . .'

On the right: the Second Presbyterian Church, after the great Chicago Fire of 1871

THE WRITERS and artists of the nineteenth century liked to think of the Hudson River as 'the American Rhine'. This beautiful valley became the best show-case of romantic revival architecture, with hundreds of castellated mansions, Gothic cottages, and Tuscan villas (the latter style is known in the U.S. as 'Hudson River Bracketed'). There are even such extravaganzas as an arms dealer's baronial castle on an island, a painter's Persian villa, and a tea merchant's domed octagonal house with touches of chinoiserie.

The Gothic delight shown above, with a dozen gables, clustered chimneys, barge-boards, and diamond-paned windows, was the gatekeeper's lodge of an estate at Poughkeepsie. 'The Little Pink House' was moved in 1962 to save it from the bulldozer.

80

FULL-BLOWN Gothic mansions were rare. Belmead, the 1845 'Tudor' home of a Virginia planter, boasted 'almost every kind of window used at the period to which the style belongs—the triple lancet, the arched, the square headed, the bay, the oriel, and the triangular. There are three or four varieties of gables, with buttresses and turrets, and an air of originality and boldness is bestowed upon the whole composition by the great tower, serving to give a pyramidal and artistical form to the whole pile of building.' However, such costly cut stone could be translated into 'Carpenter Gothic' and the Gothic tracery became the fretsaw work known as gingerbread. The 'English Cottage' below was built in 1849 for $2,800.

The country homes of a New York banker (*above*) and merchant (*below*)

The so-called Wedding Cake House (*above*) is a four-square Maine home which was made fashionable by added Gothic trim and pinnacles. The story about the sea-captain who gave it to his bride instead of a wedding cake is a tourist-trade legend.

Oak Bluffs on the island of Martha's Vineyard is a seaside resort of colourful cottages, founded in the 1830s as a Methodist 'Camp Meeting Ground'.

EASTERN fashions came late to the Far West of the United States and lingered on for years. These two vaguely Gothic houses on the Pacific Coast date from the 'eighties.

The bizarre mansion above, built for William Carson in Northern California, has become famous as the epitome of Victorian ostentation. Carson was the owner of redwood forests and sawmills and may have wanted to display the wonderful things that could be done with lumber.

A SOUTHERN California house offering
a fantastic mixture of architectural
motifs. Note the strange tower, the
Mogulesque dome, shingles, spindle-
work, and 'Chinese' railing.

ALL KINDS OF

Scroll Sawing 2 Wood Turning.

— AND —

ARCHITECTURAL CARVING,

Done to Order, at Short Notice.

The gingerbread arches of a farmhouse (*left*), a cemetery
gate (*above*), and a seaside hotel (*below*).

Left and right:
Three houses at
Port-au-Prince,
the capital of
Haiti, which has
hundreds of
Victorian villas,
no two of them
alike.

THE most fanciful wooden vernacular design of the nineteenth century is found in the West Indies. Standing under a tropical sky, in gardens of brilliant flowers, painted in garish hues, inhabited by men of colour, these houses give the delightfully exaggerated effect of stage sets.

Right: Verandah screen on the island of Saint Croix.

The ancient fable about the descent of Gothic architecture from tree growth was still credited in the nineteenth century, and the Gothic Revival is closely intertwined with the art of gardening. This hexagonal pavilion was built to shelter a park guard. The lady below is undoubtedly keeping a tryst; the 'summer house' was a favourite spot for unchaperoned romance among the Victorians.

The pleasure dome above is a conservatory in San Francisco's Golden Gate Park.
elow is the graceful vinery of Philip S. Van Rensselaer, Esq., on the Hudson River.

The subject of this romanticized painting (*c.* 1850) appears to rival the scale of the Sir Walter Scott Memorial. It is the monument to a waterworks engineer which actually stands about twelve feet high.

THE VICTORIANS' frequent visits to their many loved ones combined duty with recreation. Landscaped cemeteries were openly publicized as 'the most enchanting spot in the country', 'a charming pleasure ground', 'a scene of much resort'.

THE ENTRANCE to the famous Green-Wood cemetery in Brooklyn 'exhibits a pleasing union of firm solidity and airy grace, which marks the best specimens of Gothic art. In its sculptured pediments it presents likelife pictures of those sacred scenes, which have consoled and cheered the Christian mourner for more than eighteen hundred years.' Note the visitors on horseback.

93

CITY CHURCHES of the Gothic Revival are rather grim structures of grey granite, brown sandstone, or sooty brick. They suggest long sermons and dutiful observance of the Sabbath. But the wooden country churches are a delight; there seems to be an unintentional touch of whimsy about their endless variety of local craftsmanship. Most of them are really constructed in the traditional American 'Carpenter Georgian' which has been made into Carpenter Gothic by a few pointed windows, crockets, and finials.

THIS IS not an allegorical picture of Faith but the Floating Church of the Redeemer for Boatmen and Seamen which sat upon two 100-ton boats in the Delaware River. A model was exhibited in the American section at the Great Exhibition of 1851; the church was later moved to a conventional foundation on dry land, where it burned down in 1868.

THE CANADIAN Houses of Parliament are a masterpiece of Victorian Gothic. The buildings on a riverside bluff are enhanced by a boldly scaled array of fountains, statuary, lamps, and ironwork.

The sixteen-sided Parliamentary Library, patterned like a medieval chapter house, is strikingly picturesque both inside and out.

96

HERE ARE some examples of 'Commercial Gothic'. The Jayne Building in Philadelphia, built in 1849 for a patent medicine manufacturer, was America's first skyscraper. Although there were only seven storeys above ground and two below, the soaring façade of 'Venetian Gothic' design was an impressive sight. The building was recently torn down.

No comment is necessary on the architecture of Eli Hess' Marble Mantel Warerooms; but note the windows of the Exchange & Fairmount horse car! The Grover & Baker Sewing Machine Manufacturing Company of Boston had this unusual showroom on New York's Broadway.

99

THE AMERICAN Volunteer Fire Company was a social club as well, and the firemen sported colourful paraphernalia of flamboyant design. This San Francisco fire house was unique, with its Ruritanian Operetta

Gothic effect. The pinnacles are fireplugs and the gargoyles portraits of former fire chiefs. The building became a popular landmark but was recently razed.

Nothing quite like the interior illustrated above could be seen on land or sea. It is the saloon of the Mississippi river boat *Grand Republic*, the most splendid example of the 'Steamboat Gothic' style.

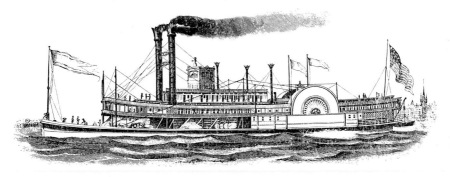

AMERICAN GOTHIC furniture has, of course, not the slightest resemblance to any real pieces of the Middle Ages. The designers simply adapted scaled-down architectural details to the job at hand. The pointed arch even appears on the sewing-machine case.

The chairs opposite were designed by the famous Gothic Revival architects Alexander Jackson Davis and James Renwick.

The 'parlour organs', which suggest miniature buildings, show the transatlantic influence of Charles Locke Eastlake, the celebrated author of *Hints on Household Taste*.

MUSEUM OF THE CITY OF NEW YORK   SMITHSONIAN INSTITUTION

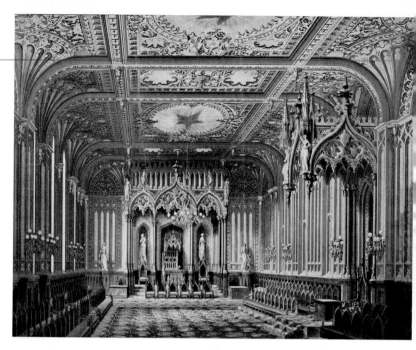

THE SUMPTUOUS Grand Lodge Room of the Philadelphia Masonic Hall. The pinnacled building is no more, but the furnishings, with their serried ranks of Gothic seats, are now in the 'Gothic Hall of the Sir Knights' of the present Masonic Temple.

Charles Oakford & Sons,

Wholesale and Retail Dealers and Manufacturers of
HATS, CAPS, AND FURS.

THE ELEGANT lithograph of Oakford's Hat Store includes a portrait of the proprietor (third from left). Here we see an early appearance of that perennial interior decorators' favourite—the blank shield.

NEW ORLEANS is famous for its
lace-like cast-iron galleries

WHAT IS this curious iron tabernacle in a public square? A drinking fountain erected by the Sons of Temperance in 1876.

GOTHIC ORNAMENT was translated into cast iron on a massive scale. American foundries offered thousands of patterns ('railings, gratings, verandahs, balconies, furniture, statuary, settees, chairs, mantels, wash-stands, toilet-glasses, centre tables, tree guards, fountains, brackets, crestings, bannerets, finials, and crosses').

AFTER DECADES of neglect and derision the American Gothic house has been rediscovered. Indeed it may be considered to be the spiritual home of that genius of *The New Yorker*, Chas. Addams.

108

This is the End.

CANAL BOAT

BAROQUE

BY JOHN O'CONNOR

AS A minor remnant of the decorative luxury of the early nineteenth century, canal narrow-boat painting has passed during the last ten years from a highly personal to a more formal popular art. The small, often very appealing panels on the cabin walls inside and outside the narrow boat have an affinity with the roses of the eighteenth-century boudoirs in France and Austria and the hand-painted Viennese pottery of the same period.

13

IN BRILLIANT green, scarlet, yellow, and pale blue, the landscape and flower pictures are painted in a tradition as rigid as a Gothic screen. Black is used as a foil to white cord in ship-shape order. These decorations are as incongruous in the setting of an English landscape, hedgerow, weed, and dark water, as a flowered teapot at a picnic. Cheap fairing pieces of china in the 1880s may be the direct source of inspiration for these designs, recalling as they do the crowded mantelpieces and corner cupboards of a Victorian midland cottage. This parody of the china cabinet of the 'Big House' rising from the ashes of burnt palaces of eighteenth-century France, apparently became a necessity to the travelling comfort of the boatmen of the English canals.

115

CANAL BOAT decoration is more severe and generally smaller in scale and form than that of the gypsy caravan. The shape of the boat itself, built for narrow bridges, tunnels, and wharves, denies excesses and frills. Canal boats in the 1960s still use a formal pattern of décor, in the style of road transport vehicles, and the rose and castle of the water bucket now have a strangely insecure position on the shelves of some departmental stores, although a few are still to be seen on the canals.

119

English Suburban

BY OLIVE COOK

PHOTOGRAPHS BY EDWIN SMITH

IT IS impossible to decide what part of England this might be. A signpost at what appears to be a main crossing points the way only to a Dog and Cat Home. Hopefully I search for a clue in the buildings. There is nothing that could be a municipal centre or place of work, there is neither church nor inn, not even a shop in sight, only a haphazard lay-out of little houses stretching away in every direction. The tiled roofs, the red, purple-brown, or salmon-coloured bricks, the rough-cast now and then covering a whole façade but more often applied only to an upper storey, announce no particular locality. They might equally well denote the fringes of Leeds or Leicester, Lowestoft or Liverpool.

If the curious pargetting on a pair of swelling bays, an indeterminate spattering of scrolls and blurred heraldic shields, remotely recalls the ornament on Sparrowe's House, Ipswich, the pitchy branching timbers crammed into twin gables on the opposite side of the road could be taken for enfeebled cousins of Welsh border country black-and-white work, while a few yards farther on a neat band of vertical fish-scale tiles fitted between top and bottom bays presents a stilted mechanical version of a tradition peculiar to Kent, Surrey, and Sussex. To add to the confusion the next two villas sport isolated areas of clap-boarding over the front doors and are fronted by low ragged-topped walls of emphatically pointed Cotswold limestone.

The materials of which these houses are constructed counterfeit those of every region. What of the shapes they have been made to assume? Again all is confusion, a single road offering an assortment of ill-digested details from almost every period style grafted on to a basic semi-detached, two-storeyed, bay-windowed plan. Even a pair of villas of flat-roofed glass and concrete conform to the general design.

Sometimes the square or polygonal bays of a couple of dwellings rise up side by side, sometimes it is the two front doors which rub shoulders, flinging the big windows to either end of the double façade. One such façade is separated by a moulded string course into an upper half of pebble-dash and a lower floor of pink brick. At either end octagonal bays jut into small front plots. The square-headed wooden casements of the bedroom storey are plain, while those below are filled with leaded lights, making a pattern of pointed arcading in the Gothic manner. A disproportionately generous square window occupies almost all the wall space above each door. And the doors, divided from one another by a neat privet hedge, exactly alike except that one is painted cream, the other green, are even more curious in style than the rest of the building. Six cushiony panels are surmounted by a glass roundel encircled by vaguely art nouveau, spoon-shaped depressions and flanked by leaded oval windows set in broad deeply moulded frames. A wide shelf projects from the lintel apparently held up by two massive iron chains fastened to the wall on either side of a mock-Georgian fanlight which seems to sit on the shelf.

Front doors exhibit more diversity than any other single feature. Here are a pair sheltered by tiled, round-arched brick porches, while their neighbours in more substantial villas probably of rather earlier date peep through Moorish arches of variegated brick reminiscent of those often used with such gusto by the Victorians in conjunction with Early English or Decorated. These are followed by a brace of steep-roofed, wood-framed entrances, and immediately after them come two cream-coloured doors of faintly Georgian aura except that to the left of the one and to the right of the other there bulges a triangular oriel adorned with stained-glass peacocks. Limed, studded oak next meets the eye, fitted with conspicuous latches and spidery ironwork.

To look from here across the road to a pair of metal-framed doors consisting of plain, asymmetrically disposed lozenges of glass should, the reader might imagine, evoke a thrilling sense of contrast. But in fact it induces nothing but a flat recognition of spurious antiquity on the one hand and sham de Stijl on the other.

A glance inside these houses confirms the impression given by the exteriors. Beamed ceilings, latched doors, brick-nogging in the chimney-piece, here and there conjure up a phoney cottage atmosphere. False, electrically reddened coals glow beneath meagre imitation Jacobean mantelpieces, or chunks of pastel-coloured tiles form kerbs and fireside seats and mount in steps towards a crowning ledge to support the domestic gods—objects ranging from crest china and crinoline ladies to cubist vases, angular glassware, and Alsatian dogs, according to the age of the owners. The same factor decides whether the 'three-piece' in the lounge shall be 'rustic', sprung, padded and rounded, spiky, or assertively boxy, whether the dining-room be 'period' or 'modern', whether a border shall run beneath the picture-rail over a plain, spotted, striped, or jazz wallpaper and whether one wall shall be patterned and the other three plain.

In nearly every house, however, there are two rooms which are unpretentious, almost devoid of make-believe and well suited to their purpose: the bathroom and the kitchen. The amenities provided by these rooms are not part of the 'styles' on which the design of the rest of the house is based, and although baths and tiles tend to assume rosy, lemon-yellow, leaf-green, and ebon hues, efficiency, as with the owner's car, seems important and acceptable where no tradition exists to arouse false sentiment.

Apart from the 'usual offices', the main characteristic of these homes, both within and without, is a depressing air of unreality. The distinction between past and present, between town and country, has utterly broken down. Although the residential pairs are surrounded by little gardens and hedged in from the road, there is nothing rural about them. Nature is here more trimmed and tamed, more cabined and confined, than in a London square. The most frequently occurring tree is the acid pink alien almond; crazy-paving leads from gate to porch, meanders across minute, immaculate lawns, and zigzags about geometric rose-beds; plaster rabbits bob up from the bulbs; gnomes crouch on rockeries and perch on bird-baths; and a dwarf concrete windmill stands among mathematically spaced salvias.

Yet the whole district is redolent of a dimly felt nostalgia for the country. The roads are the antithesis of town streets. Not only do they contain no repeating units, no terraces planned as architectural wholes, but they are seldom quite straight, they often become cul-de-sacs, and footpaths are sometimes of shingle, edged with grass and ornamental trees.

The roads are rarely called by that name; *Place, Crescent,*

Square, and of course *Terrace* are avoided, while *Street* is never used. Instead *Drive*, *Avenue*, *Way*, *Close*, *Grove*, *Chase*, and *Ride* conspire to excite rural memories of a suitably elevated kind. This effect is strengthened in many cases by the names of the individual houses: The Leys, Berrymead, The Garth (in oxydized Gothic lettering on a metal-framed door of yellow, opaque glass), The Barn, Dormers (though there are none to be seen), and Pantiles.

Like the architecture, these road and house names bear no relation to their actual geographical situation; nor do they commemorate local personalities, local traditions, local activities or landmarks, as do the names of country buildings and town streets. When they are not affectedly countrified (Oakhill Grove, Woodland Ride, Beech Way) the roads may be called after popular heroes or film stars (Mollison Avenue, Valentino Way), create an ambience of gentility (Beverley Drive, Chatsworth Grove), or of high romance, whether of place (California Close) or period (Queen Edith's Way).

The house names, when not of rural connotation, celebrate the scene of a successful holiday or idyllic honeymoon (Trescoe, Inverary, Countisbury, Capri) or consist of words either coined from the Christian names of the happily married owners (Davmay, Chanan, Philmar) or perpetuate some laboured jest or banality (Dunromin, Restawhile). The number, unaccompanied by a name, is hardly ever found, and then it is given an arty twist. *One 2 Six* appears in bold Egyptian characters on a wooden gate framing an optimistic rising sun, and *Forty-Nine* slopes in thin metal italic across a flimsy iron gate describing a crossword-puzzle pattern in the air.

Amusing though some of these incongruous details may be at first glance to an impartial observer, they never make the sharp impact of Victorian domestic architecture, which is equally composite. They do not produce the delighted shock of the simple stuccoed rectangles of the early period embroidered with Gothic or Oriental trimmings; nor have they the conviction of the later massive, picturesque piles which so robustly combine English medieval openings with French Renaissance turrets and Tudor chimney-stacks.

Victorian villas of these kinds are found in the earliest of the suburbs—places like Bayswater, South and West

Hampstead, Streatham, and Gipsy Hill—and they certainly influenced modern suburbia. They first embodied the idea of the single or semi-detached house built in a garden, without regard for street design, in a strictly residential area. They first introduced the custom of giving an arbitrarily chosen name to a house which already had a perfectly adequate number. But there is no real continuity between Victorian and twentieth-century suburban architecture. A Victorian villa wholeheartedly reflects the precise style and taste of its age. The twentieth-century suburban house, on the other hand, is never entirely of its own time. If it follows contemporary fashion it does so timidly, fifteen or twenty years late. If it harks back to the more distant past, as it mostly does, the essentials are so feebly grasped, interpreted with so little fantasy, that accurate dating is almost impossible.

The suburban style took its departure not so much from the Victorian outskirts of the larger cities as from the planned garden suburbs which began to come into existence towards the end of the nineteenth century. Bedford Park, begun in 1875, had already started a new trend with its red brick, tile-hung gables, white casement windows, quaint oriels, and cosy porches, details which are common in all the suburban areas which developed during the first forty years of this century and which still occur with surprising frequency. The open plan, the allusions to rural traditions in places like Bedford Park, sprang from a reaction against the hideous, uniform terraces in working-class districts, where the thousands who had been driven from the land by the industrial revolution were forced to spend squalid lives. Modern suburbia has a similar origin.

As a style, Suburban seems to defy classification in the sense of the earlier architectural modes; yet, like them, it is the expression of a state of mind. It is born of a longing, anaemic and sentimental though it may be, for the sight and touch of growing nature—a traditional, normal longing that in our swollen cities has been frustrated and distorted. It represents the ordinary Englishman's instinctive horror of the human warrens of hard, clean glass, steel and concrete in which the town-planner would have him pass his days. It is his pitiful substitute for a lost rural existence, the materialization of his fundamental desire for a little place of his own.

125

The suburban scene.

THE late Victorian mixture of historic and traditional styles and the use of the name in a street of numbered houses inspired twentieth-century suburban practice, though the robust precision of Victorian example gradually gave way to feeble suggestions.

BELMONT ROAD. BROADSTAIRS.

INTERIOR and exteriors *c.* 1910. The ornamental details top right and below consciously evoke rural associations, hinting at a lane rather than a road.

THE tree-lined road and the casements, bushy front gardens and picturesque chimney-stacks are part of a garden suburb plan begun as early as 1875. They set a fashion which has been followed in suburbia ever since.

THESE leaded lights, the half-timber and rustic
porch belong to the early years of the century
but already illustrate the marked tendency of
the suburban mode to recall the farm and cottage.

AT THE top of the pages are typical suburban vistas; on the left the 'sunbeam' gate, a frequently occurring optimistic motif. The peacock theme, adapted to ironwork or the stained-glass panel of a front door, is also a favourite.

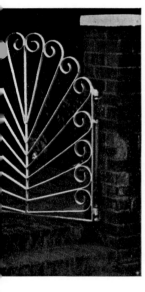

Right: front garden lay-out
and ornament.

ROGUES

and

Vagabonds

The Robin Hood Mystery

BY JOHN PITT

HODSON, HOBSON, Hudson: what have they in common?
If Mr Robert Graves is accurate in his scholarship (and this
writer would never question it) then the ancestry of these
most English of English names may be traceable to an
illicit love stolen in the green-shaded half-light of an English
forest. Hodson, Hobson, Hudson—sons of Hood, of Robin
Hood, the heroic prototype of yeoman English stock.

But here we must pause.

In 1510 the printer Wynken de Worde published a folio
headed *Here begynneth a Lyttel geste of Robyn hode*. It ran
to thirty-two quarto pages, and on its title page was depicted
the famous outlaw with Little John, holding in his hand a
quarter-staff and clad in what was most surely Lincoln
Green. As a publication it was in no sense a best-seller as we
might understand the term. But to those who could read, or
listen, it summarized not only the exploits of a legendary

and heroic figure but also those qualities which were, and still are, the pride of every man who would have the world know him as an independent character of steadfastness and strength.

It is extraordinary that such an obscure person should, even then, have existed for so long, and have been so widely known, as to have captured the interest of a medieval biographer, in much the same way that King Arthur had attracted the attention of Malory half a century earlier. (The *Geste of Robyn hode* represented the ideal yeoman to the people as the Arthurian cycle had represented the ideal knight to the upper classes.) It is even more extraordinary that this universal feeling for Robin Hood should have endured until our own time—whereas, by comparison, the interest in King Arthur has not. Who, then, was Robin Hood, and when did he live, and what manner of man was he that Hodsons, Hobsons, and Hudsons should figure so prominently in our population?

For the answer—or some of the answer—we must go to mythology. It is a commonplace that all primitive peoples have worshipped certain forces of nature which they have personalized into human form. Such was Woden, the god of the wind, to become later in history Hod, who with Morgen, the dawn-maiden, and Toki, the spirit of frost and snow, were the principal deities of the great Aryan sun-myth. And in the semi-pagan years of early English Christianity this force, this wind-god, had been qualified into the half-comic, half-credible, restless, elusive figure of Robin Goodfellow.

Today even, as a nation with a broad streak of romance underlying our no-nonsense approach to all that cannot be resolved by hard-headed empiricism, we still have a weakness for fantasy. Shakespeare knew this, and made good use of it:

> . . . a very Shetlander among the
> gossamer-winged, dainty-limbed fairies,
> strong enough to knock all their heads

THE MERRY MEN

together; a rough, knurly-limbed, fawn-faced, shock-pated, mischievous little urchin.

He was writing of this selfsame character, of Goodfellow, the Puck of *A Midsummer Night's Dream*; and if the creator of Ariel and Queen Mab, of Oberon and Titania, was a fantasist, he was drawing from and adding to a long tradition of woodland superstition which was still half-believed by the groundlings—most of whom, like the author, were townsfolk only a generation or so removed from the environment in which the action of the fantasies took place.

Robin Goodfellow, then, was the dimly remembered pagan spirit of a medieval country folk whose soul was deeply embedded in the myth and folklore of the country-side; who, though they might now largely ascribe their manifestation and powers to the Devil, nevertheless believed in sprites and pixies, gnomes and elves, the fairies and hob-goblins which lurked deep in the forest, out of sight and beyond the jurisdiction of man. *Hob*goblins! Hob. Hod. Hood. Robin Hood? Alas, it is not quite so straightforward. Another figure has made a claim, one who first comes to our notice at the beginning of the seventeenth century. His name was Robin Fitzsooth.

In 1601 was published a work entitled *The Downfall of Robert Earle of Huntingdon, afterwards called Robin Hood*. It was a tragedy in verse by the two dramatists Munday and Chettle, and it related how the Earl, a nobleman of long Saxon lineage, had been defrauded of his inheritance under the Norman domination. By way of revenge, he had retired from the society of lawful men, and had gathered together a band of retainers from the groups of freebooters, discharged soldiers, and die-hard Saxons who lurked in the forests of England at this time. The family name of the Huntingdons was Fitzsooth, and the Earl, perhaps to allay the mistrust and disapproval which so Norman a name would arouse in his followers, discarded the Fitz and became good plain Saxon Sooth—Robin Sooth, later to elide into the name by which the outlaw has been known throughout the centuries. All of which points to very little were it not for a curious entry discovered last century in the Rolls of Edward II.

But here, for a moment, we must again digress.

In our boyhood versions of the adventures of Robin— all based, of course, on the original *Geste*—there is that episode in which King Richard the Lionheart, back from the Crusades, hearing of this man whose brazen disrespect for authority had made ridicule of both Church and State, sets out alone into the forest, disguised as a friar, in the hope of encountering Robin and judging him for himself. The word is passed round that an incautious churchman is wandering through the greenwood, and in the twang of a bowstring he is encompassed by a jolly band of outlaws, all eager in their anticipation of an intensive (though naturally good-natured) bout of anti-clerical horseplay.

At the psychological moment Richard throws back his habit to reveal himself, 'The King!', the red cross of St George (one can see it in the coloured illustrations of the time) blazing out from the breastplate of his lustrous armour.

ROBIN HOOD AND THE BEGGAR

Robin and his men, astonished and mortified, beseech the royal pardon, which they obtain, but only by their promise to mend their ways and work henceforward as honest men in the service of the Sovereign. (Later they tire of the humdrum sophistication of court life, obtain their discharge, and return to the forest.)

Now in 1323 Edward II made a journey north for the purpose of visiting the royal forests, and of spending Christmas at Kenilworth with his old enemy the Earl of Lancaster. His route then, as now, passed along Watling Street, and at one point it skirted a stretch of Barnsdale Forest, notorious as a place of ambush by outlaws.

ROBIN HOOD AND THE TANNER

What quickens our interest is that tradition names both Barnsdale and Sherwood as the favourite haunts of Robin Fitzsooth. If Fitzsooth *was* Robin Hood, and if the story of the disguised King is based on fact, then it is exciting to note that Fitzsooth was reputed to be living at this time, and in the Edwardian Rolls for that year is the item: '5s.' (equivalent now to £5) payable as a *discharge* wage to a certain Robin Hode.

Here then are two possible identities of Robin: the shadowy Saxon earl, with his tenuous claim, and Robin Goodfellow, the capricious kelpie of Celtic myth. Nobody really knows which was 'Robin Hood'. But what we can be certain of is that the two legends blended to produce yet another Robin Hood, one whose character began to form at the beginning of the Hundred Years' War.

Crecy was the start of it; Poitiers and Agincourt were to

give it added impetus. After that brilliant French campaign by Edward III, when the range and marksmanship of the English bowmen on both occasions routed a vastly superior force, the words Crecy and Poitiers drew men together as might a brotherhood. The point of unity, the common interest, was archery. Throughout a thousand hamlets, in the years that followed, there developed a skill and enthusiasm amounting almost to obsession. On feast days, especially during the spring months, and more especially on May Day, the fields and clearings would be patterned with country folk, attracted by the dancing, the games, and the contests at the butts.

ROBIN HOOD AND GUY OF GISBORNE

There can be little doubt that here, at this time, and during these occasions, was blended into one all-embracing legend the character of *Hob* (who with *Morgen* and *Toki* became the Robin, Marian, and Tuck of the Morris dances) with that of the Robin Hood of the accumulated romances of medieval tradition—all now to be cast in a new mould shaped by the growing sense of vigour, yeoman worth, and national pride which had begun to suffuse the meaning of the era, and which in time gave new expression to the outlaw's character.

Moreover, two traditional figures in Lincoln Green always led those archers to the butts. And if the pagan rites of spring were not performed with the full ritual of former days, the feeling for them was there for sure in the blood of the main participants. Robin and Little John might claim the prize for the truest bow. They also claimed the affection of their warmest admirers. And Hobsons and Johnsons the world over may well trace their ancestry not to Robin Goodfellow, nor to the Earl of Huntingdon, but to the warm response to the gleam of an eye that beckoned forestwards one mellow English May Day evening many years ago.

Robin Hood: shrewd, genial, chivalrous, courageous, a natural peasant gentleman with a keen sense of sportsmanship and fair play—that is our present concept of him. Yet somehow one senses that it is a softened, genteel version, carefully spring-cleaned for the impressionable minds of persons of tender age.

Two things killed that earlier and, in a sense, more accurate assessment of Robin's character. One was the Reformation, brought in by virtue of those very qualities of which the English yeoman boasted—a pride, confidence, and shrewdness now mingled into the new religion of nationalism. The other, quite naturally, was the ousting of the long-bow by the musket. And, also, to hasten the death of the stricken myth came a new type of English Sunday, introduced by the Roundheads—yeomen farmers almost to a man. Thus the elusive, heroic, romantic Robin was displaced by the solid, florid figure of the young John Bull. Robin still turns up in the ballads and song sheets of the 1600s. In the following century he appears once or twice looking very Turpinesque with blunderbuss and tricorn hat. Dr Burney composed a musical entertainment about him in 1751, produced by the Society of the Temple of Apollo, with words by a certain Mr Moses Mendez. There was even a comic opera written about him. But ultimately, with the publication in 1791 of

ROBIN HOOD AND QUEEN KATHARINE

ROBIN HOOD AND LITTLE JOHN

Ritson's *Collection of all the ancient poems, songs, and ballads now extant relative to that outlaw To which are prefixed historical anecdotes of his life*, he passes out of public view into the realm of scholarship. The myth had ceased to grow, and the champion of medieval England seemed bound for extinction.

But that was to have reckoned without the Romantic Movement. In 1822 that eccentric and life-long friend of Shelley, Thomas Love Peacock, came across a copy of Ritson's definitive collection. It so enthralled him that he resolved to write a medieval romance of the greenwood, basing his plot on episodes as recounted in the *Geste*. So he began his satirical, sunny-natured, slightly Rabelaisian *Maid Marian*. Its completion was delayed by illness, and before it could finally appear Sir Walter Scott, to whom also the *Geste* had spoken across the centuries, had produced *Ivanhoe*, which, though it depicts Robin in a minor role, perhaps recaptures the spirit and fable of the greenwood better than anything ever written. *Ivanhoe*, as well as stimulating an antiquarian passion for archery, also renewed literary interest in the Robin Hood legend. And Scott's representation of life around the greenwood tree, his characterization and stirring dialogue, firmly set the style for a school of 'quoth he' writers that has lasted up to present times.

So, into the romantic literature of the early nineteenth century, Robin emerged from a long winter of oblivion, from an era of enlightened objectivity which had blunted the natural edge of his countryman's Celtic disposition for romance and twilight fantasy. Today he still lives, but as a changed Robin, a 'justified' Robin, a romantic, unurbanized figure vaguely epitomizing the city-dweller's yen for clean, uncomplicated, mildly exciting, but essentially unattainable living. Translated into modern terms his adventures might be said to represent the struggle between good and evil which seem to require personification in even the most sophisticated of us.

In this he has recently been joined by a number of companions: Billy the Kid, Davy Crockett, William Tell, Dick Turpin, and other rogues of history, who by some paradox have become the self-appointed champions of the underprivileged. But to an Englishman the noblest and boldest is Robin Hood of Sherwood. Courageous, gentle, strong, steadfast, *our* man, we remind ourselves, has been placing his shots around the greenwood for nigh on a thousand years.

The engraving above and those decorating the first four pages of this essay are from early broadside ballads in the British Museum. The other engravings are by Thomas Bewick.

150

wm Shon Catti

Y JOHN MOORE

THEY CALL Twm Shon Catti the Welsh Robin Hood; but apart from the fact that both men were robbers they seem to have been as different as their two nations are different—yet I, an Englishman, confess that I prefer this cheerful rogue Twm. There's something a little bit too-good-to-be-true about Robin Hood. I've always wished that Shaw, who loved pulling English legs, had written a play about him; for he was the quintessential English hero, almost public school. Within three centuries our singers of songs and tellers of tales had turned a dubious outlaw into a do-gooder who robbed the rich in order to sustain the poor, a chivalrous and romantic lover of Maid Marian, a sound Christian whose exploits had the approval of a jolly decent fat friar, and—to make sure he was sufficiently U—an Earl of Huntingdon in disguise!

Twm Shon Catti's legend, on the other hand, has none of these polite trimmings. He entirely lacked Robin Hood's chivalry (or damned respectability, as some might term it). When he stole it was for his own benefit, not for the poor; and his motives were the simple ones, that he needed the money, and that thieving was fun. (Perhaps it was also a national pastime—'Taffy was a Welshman, Taffy was a thief'.) Maid Marian, I fancy, wouldn't have been safe for half an hour in the greenwood with Twm; and since he was certainly anti-clerical and had a particular detestation of monks, there would have been no chubby Friar Tuck handy to help him make an honest woman of her. Twm, let's admit it, was as rough, wild, and unpredictable as the winds that blew down from his own rough mountains: cattle-rustling, cheating, cozening, night-prowling, hard-riding, hard-drinking, and, I don't doubt, 'given to fornications, and to taverns, and sack, and wine, and metheglins, and to drinkings, and swearings, and starings, pribbles and prabbles'—in the words of his fellow Welshman Parson Evans. It is true that he turned over a new leaf in the end and was appointed (on the principle of 'set a thief to catch a thief', perhaps?) High Sheriff of Carmarthenshire. But that is the end of the story. Let us start at the beginning.

Twm Shon Catti was born, then, about the year 1530, somewhere near the town of Tregaron in Cardiganshire, a place famous in those days for its excellent hams, but famous now for Twm Shon Catti. Some say he was the natural son of a knight called Sir John Wynne of Gwedyr by a young woman called Catherine Jones, while others heatedly argue that his father was John-the-son-of-David-ap-Madog-ap-Howel-Moetheu by Catherine-a-natural-daughter-of-Meredydd-ap-Ieuan. Either version may be true, for Twm o'Sion a Catti means simply Tom the son of John and Catherine. He was certainly illegitimate, and he became known as Tom Jones.

As a boy, he was always in trouble for his pranks and his mischief. When he was still in his teens he 'adopted the profession of a thief', as George Borrow rather portentously puts it, and before long he had set himself up very nicely as the most successful stealer of cattle and horses in the whole of West Wales. He devoted to his chosen profession much skill and cunning, daring, impudence, wit, and a fine sense of the ridiculous; in fact he cocked a snook at the world, getting his own back, perhaps, for his misfortune of bastardy. *Why brand they us as base?* he might have cried,

> Who in the lusty stealth of Nature take
> More composition and fierce quality
> Than doth within a dull, stale, tired bed
> Go to the creating a whole tribe of fops
> Got 'tween asleep and wake . . .

Unlike Edgar, however, he doesn't seem to have had a chip on his shoulder at all. There never was a better-humoured rogue; and the humble people loved him for his jests and doubtless sympathized with him for being born on the wrong side of the blanket and losing a patrimony thereby.

You must understand that cattle-stealing was by no means a dishonourable profession in those parts of Wales during the sixteenth century. The native inhabitants had only just been granted equality with Englishmen before the law; and they were probably still unaware of this inestimable privilege since by the Acts of Union the courts had to be conducted in English—without the benefit of interpreters! The Welsh, being anarchic by nature, had no great respect for English justice administered by Englishmen or by Welsh stooges in a language which they didn't like or understand. So if a man's profession of cattle-stealer set him agin the Englishman's law, good luck to him—so long as he didn't steal one's own cattle! I imagine the inhabitants of Tregaron had much the same attitude to Twm—one of amused admiration for his daring and his cheek—as they had during the early part of the present century for the poachers on the rivers of mid-Wales. These strong streams from the high mountains, with their turbulent rapids and deep, clear pools (where incidentally the last beavers in Britain built their dams when William the Conqueror was King), were noted for salmon and sewin. The fishing rights had been bought up by well-fed Englishmen, but most of the salmon were caught by hungry Welshmen who fished for food as well as for fun. The English brought Scottish gillies and even, with shocking effrontery, toughs from Prussia, to guard the banks of their rivers; and the Welsh therefore pushed in those Scots and Huns, and held them under until they damned near drowned, which actions were regarded sympathetically by most of the inhabitants, including the local bobbies and magistrates.

Twm Shon Catti's escapades were likewise approved by the majority of his countrymen. And of course they grew more marvellous in the telling, so that there were soon as many legends about him as we have concerning Robin Hood. Welshmen are great tellers of tales, and I'm not going to cross my heart and spit on the floor and swear to the absolute truth, in every trifling particular and meticulous detail, of the tales about Twm Shon Catti which they recite in their pubs after market. For these things happened a great while ago; there has been a good deal of beer drunk since then; and beer, as we know, is apt to make a long tale longer. All the same, he'd be a brave man who would dare to doubt, after market in a Tregaron pub, the fantastical story, for instance, of the short-tailed bull, which takes about fifteen minutes by the clock over the fireplace in the bar. There are men in Tregaron who could lead you to the village of Newton and show you the very field, on the right-hand side about a mile beyond the bridge at Brecon, where the farmer kept this short-tailed bull: about three hundred and fifty years ago!

But a Welsh tale runs no straighter than a Welsh river.

Well, now, Twm Shon Catti catches sight of this bull, see, as he's riding home all the way from London town.

And why had he been to London? Well, it was prudent, see, for him to be absent from Tregaron for a little while. Farmer called Roberts from Ysbyty-Ystwyth took it into his head our Twm had stolen a bullock out of his stall. Came riding into Tregaron in a terrible way about it. Outside Twm's house he sees an old beggar huddled on the pavement.

'Does Twm Shon Catti live here?'

'Yes,' says the beggar.

The farmer throws him a coin. 'Then hold my horse while I go in and speak to the rascal.'

He hands the beggar his whip too—armed to the teeth he is, and he holds a pistol in each hand as he goes roaring and raging into the house of Twm Shon Catti.

But as soon as the farmer's inside, this dirty old beggar stops scratching his fleas, throws off his threadbare cloak, jumps into the saddle, and gallops away to the house of that damned suspicious fellow whose bullock he'd stolen a few days before. Great chap for disguise was Twm, and on the way he takes off his false beard and washes his face in a stream, so that he's looking real chapel-respectable when he knocks at the door and tells the farmer's wife: 'Your husband's in great trouble, lady, and he needs fifty pounds to get him out of it. Look, here's the whip he gave me to show that I had his authority to ask you for the money that'll keep him out of gaol.' The wife, of course, knows the horse and recognizes the whip, so she hands Twm the fifty pounds, with one extra for himself to recompense his trouble. Off rides Twm, all the way to London, where he sells the horse and spends all the money and makes a lot of young ladies happy before he thinks it's time he came home.

And there he is, look now, riding home by Newton when he sees this short-tailed bull! By damn, says Twm, never seen the like of such a beast before; and steal it I will before next Brecon market. He goes home, and makes a very fine tail, 'twould take a veterinary surgeon straight from college to tell the difference between this and a real tail. One dark night he rides to Newton and steals the bull and sticks the new tail on to its little stump. Come market day, he takes it into town.

'Very fine bull,' cries he, 'who'll buy my fine bull?'

A crowd gathers round, and before long out steps the farmer who owns the bull, shaking his stick and shouting: 'That's the spit image of my bull, which a damned thief stole out of the field on Tuesday.'

'Can you swear to the bull?' says Twm, cheeky-like.

'Well, I could swear to it on the Bible, see, but for the tail of it. Mine had a very short tail, but this one's tail is very long. I would like to find out,' says the farmer, looking nasty at Twm, 'whether this be a real tail or no?'

'You would?' shouts Twm. 'Then by damn so you shall!' And he pulls out a sharp knife and cuts off the bull's tail a little way above where the false tail is fixed on to it. 'So it's your bull?' says Twm, roaring with laughter, as the stump drips blood and the poor bull bellows. 'And I put a false tail on it, did I? I think you should beg my pardon, and buy the bull off me at ten pounds, for doubting the word of an honest man.'

Well, the crowd backs up Twm, see, and before long the farmer is forced to pay ten pounds for his short-tailed bull, which now has a tail even shorter. The farmer, as he leads it away, calls to Twm:

'Won't you give me the tail, for my wife to make a bowl of soup?'

'Not I,' laughs Twm. 'I'll keep it against the time I steal another bull with a short tail——' and he runs away before the farmer can catch him.

Twm was by no means the only lawless fellow in the wild Wales of the fifteen-hundreds. The few roads which ran between the hills were plagued by highwaymen; and since there was little fellowship among thieves, the cattle-stealer who rode alone, and whose purse was likely to be heavy with his ill-gotten gains, was obviously a tempting prey for them. Being held up by one of these gentry, Twm pretended to be a great coward, and said he was ready to hand over his leather bag which was full of gold coins. 'There's only one thing that I beg of you,' pleaded Twm, trembling like a man with the palsy. 'I would not like it to be said that the famous

Twm Shon Catti surrendered without a fight. If I give you my money will you put a pistol-shot through my hat, so that I can show my friends in Tregaron what a great battle there was between us before you overcame me?' The highwayman was much amused by the craven behaviour of one who had such a reputation for courage, and told him to hold up his hat in his hand. Neatly he put a bullet-hole through it. 'Now just one more, if you'll be so good,' said Twm, 'to make it a better tale!' The highwayman, laughing, pulled out his second pistol and drilled another hole through Twm's hat, close as if they were two peas in a pod.

'Thank you very much indeed,' said Twm politely, drawing his own pistol and taking good aim. The highwayman, having discharged both his weapons, was now at his mercy; and Twm shot him dead, took his fine horse and his purse (which was crammed with the money he'd just stolen from a rich traveller), and rode happily home to Tregaron.

So in the stories quick-witted Twm pops up here, there, and everywhere, always ready with tricks and disguises—an old beggar-woman, a crippled soldier, a grave clergyman— always pulling the legs of his victims, making fools of them, teasing them as he robs them. Gaily he rides his fast horses along the trails among the lonely hills—and he can afford the fastest, for he generally steals them! Gaily he courts the girls, drinks with his cronies, persecutes the fat Abbot of Tally who was his pet aversion and principal foe, even raids the monastery and steals the best of the monks' Old Ale! He is surely one of the gayest rogues in legend or history— save only when he is making up poetry, when Twm, being a true Welshman, is always extremely sad. Now I come to think of it, I do not know any Welsh verse that is really light-hearted or merry; in order to be a bard in Wales you have to put on a cloak of melancholy. And Twm did become a bard, according to one story; he was so ordained in 1564 at an eisteddfod at Llandaff.

So when he rode alone among the wild, sad hills Twm made up the kind of poems which bards, being grave men, are accustomed to write, very solemn and moral poems, and on sacred themes rather than profane ones. One day he wrote a whole Ode to Sorrow, *Ciwyd y Gofid*, which I asked my friend Mr J. G. Thomas to translate for me. This is how it begins:

I have a rascally companion who follows me like a spectral foe; He is called Care . . .

and Twm goes on to say that Care is always with him wherever he is riding, and that Care is generally accompanied by his eldest son, called Debt, and by his wife Anxiety, and by his daughter Want. 'That is the family that possesses me daily without let up. Wrestling with Care I suffer trouble after trouble, fall after fall, and he's the victor. . . .'

So wrote Twm, in beautiful Welsh verses composed in impeccable metres, and sad enough to satisfy a whole convocation of bards; and he finished very piously and properly:

There is a Lord over us all. . . . He'll strengthen Twm eventually, and aid him to reach that home where all good men are, having accomplished some good work in the end.

But Twm, his ode finished, probably spurred his horse and galloped off happily to steal a whole herd of cattle!

His deftness in poetry no doubt came in handy when he started courting the heiress of Ystrad-Fin; for George Borrow says that Twm could 'treat a lady to penillion about her face and her ankle and the tip of her ear'. He must have spent a great many such stanzas upon the lady of Ystrad-Fin, who lived in a grand house and was heiress to the whole of a green and pleasant valley, that of the Towy; for although Twm was a very handsome fellow and (according to some stories) had once saved her from a highwayman who held up her carriage, she was naturally disinclined to marry a thief. When poetry failed him Twm resorted to a characteristic stratagem. He rode one day to Ystrad-Fin and standing beneath the lady's window begged her to come out; he was off to the wars in France, he explained, and wanted to say his last farewell. But she prudently remained behind her iron-barred window.

'Whatever you have to say, say it quickly, and go your way.'

Twm then said he had one final request before he left her for ever; would she not stretch her white hand through the bars so that he might impress one last kiss of love upon it?

The lady saw little harm in that, so she stretched her arm through the bars. 'There's my hand, then: kiss it once and be gone!'

Twm, seizing it firmly, said: 'Now I've got you; and I shall not let you go till you become my wife.'

'Never!' cried the beautiful lady of Ystrad-Fin.

'Then,' said Twm, drawing his sword, 'I swear I will cut off your hand unless you promise to marry me!'

What could the lady do? She was already half in love with the fearful fellow; and she certainly didn't want to lose her right hand. So she promised; and Twm, who didn't trust women's promises to last for more than a few minutes, called out of concealment the terrified priest whom he had forcibly brought along with him, and the couple were married there and then!

No more thieving for Twm Shon Catti! He was now very rich, being lord of the Fin Valley, so they made him Justice of the Peace and High Sheriff of Carmarthen, and begged him to clear the country of all the robbers, horse-stealers, cattle-rustlers, and thieves who plagued it. He set about the job with enthusiasm; and though for old times' sake Twm always gave a prisoner one last chance to reform, if he failed to do so Twm would cheerfully cry, 'Hang the rogue!' and pass on to the next case. Before long 'a child might walk through the county quite safe with a purse of gold in its hand'. And Twm lived happily and respected until he was ninety years old—or so they will tell you in the pubs at Tregaron after market, when the beer has brought the past to life again so that the exploits of Twm Shon Catti three hundred years ago seem as close and as real as if they had happened but yesterday.

Dick Turpin

BY FRANK MORLEY

WHEN A character becomes legendary one may be reasonably sure that there is some reality behind the story, on the old principle that there is no smoke without fire. But the 'reality' is not always to be found in the actual conduct of the hero so much as in some general social urge to make a hero of him. What was the urge to make a hero of Dick Turpin?

We have to agree about the scale of the legend. The legend of Dick Turpin, the highwayman, is in no sense comparable with the great legend of Robin Hood. We may know nothing about Robin Hood as an individual, or about Maid Marian or Little John, Friar Tuck, Will Scarlet, and the rest; but we don't need to know who they were in 'actuality'. They go on living in the imagination, invested with the reality of complete belief, representative (if one wishes to think about them that way) of the ancient great resistance movement of the Danelaw against a harsh and alien Norman rule. The Robin Hood legend is a great legend because it represents a permanent kick against 'the Establishment'. So also is the Arthurian legend a great legend, and to discuss the opposition of those two legends would be to discuss large spiritual elements in English history. The legend of Dick Turpin is something very much smaller, yet if it persists at all it must gather its existence from some sort of permanent interest. How should one describe that interest? Is it the perennial interest in 'Cops and Robbers'?

I have read many accounts of Dick Turpin; incomparably the best was that compiled by Arty Ash and Julius Day, published in book form as *Immortal Turpin* in 1948. There is no other study of Turpin which is so complete and scrupulous. I wish to make this general acknowledgment; I have to filch the facts from this book and rob from it with as little compunction as Turpin displayed on the highway; but at least I make apology. To you, my fences (for you now know that they are stolen goods), I pass the facts which Messrs Ash and Day earned by their own hard work.

It may be taken that Richard Turpin was born in 1705 in the village of Hempstead in Essex, seven miles or so from Saffron Walden. His father was John Turpin, a butcher, who later became landlord of the Bell Inn at Hempstead. His mother's maiden name was Maria Palmer. Dick Turpin was born at the Bell Inn; it is still standing, but now renamed the Rose and Crown. Dick was taught to read and write by the Hempstead schoolmaster, James Smith, who later on identified Turpin at the trial at York. At the age of sixteen Dick was apprenticed to a butcher in Whitechapel, but after his five years' apprenticeship returned to Essex, married one of Mr Smith's father's maids, and started in business on his own account as a butcher in Thaxted.

That brings us to about the year 1728, when Turpin was twenty-three. The business at Thaxted failed; Turpin is then heard of at Enfield, and again as a butcher at Souson (known today as Sewardstone). Our authors conjecture that Turpin's failures in business were due to his spending too much time in taverns. During the trial at York, ten years later, there is a passage in the testimony:

> COUNSEL TO MR SMITH: When you spoke to him in the Castle did you know him?
> SMITH: Yes, I did, and he did confess to know me and said, unto me two or three times, 'Let us Bung our Eyes in Drink' and I drank with him, which is this Richard Turpin.

This is an interesting greeting from a former pupil to a former schoolmaster. We may return to Mr Smith later;

at the moment it must be observed that Dick Turpin's practice as a butcher at Souson was raising another question, not whether he spent too much time in taverns but what was the source of his beef supply? Cattle in that neighbourhood had a mysterious way of disappearing. In 1733 a Mr Giles of Plaistow lost some valuable bullocks which were 'distinguished by their curious and distinctive markings'. Search of Turpin's slaughter-house while he was away from home disclosed two carcasses which seemed to tally in measurement with the missing bullocks; but the carcasses had been skinned and there were no hides on the premises. The hides were traced to a tanner at Waltham Abbey, were identifiable, and the transaction was traced back to Turpin. Mr Giles applied for a warrant for Turpin's arrest. As a result of this simple detective work, Dick Turpin took to the woods. His flight was regarded as admission of guilt.

In 1733 cattle-stealing was a hanging matter, and so long as this charge was against him Turpin might as well go in for other crimes. There are many stories, but few provable, about his actions when he was first on the run. The probability is that for a time he remained in the area of Epping Forest (an area then ten times larger than now), not altogether losing touch with his family; from time to time he remained in touch with his people for the rest (five more years) of his life. But even if he had some help from home, living rough in the forest in winter or wet weather presented nothing but a poor prospect for a lone man. A band of housebreakers known as Gregory's Gang was at that time beginning to be much talked of, with headquarters some say in Epping Forest, some say Whitechapel. The exploits of Gregory's Gang were reported in the newspapers, and the vanity of being in the newspapers was an additional incentive to the share-out of loot from the robberies with violence in which the Gang specialized. By 1735 Turpin was a member of Gregory's Gang of sufficient standing to be spoken of by name in the *London Gazette*.

On one of Turpin's first enterprises with Gregory's Gang they struck it rich. Who put the finger on a lonely farmhouse at Rippleside, near Barking, nobody knows; but the Gang arrived one night on stolen horses, battered down the door, bound the farmer, his wife, the son-in-law, and serving-maid, and stripped the place. They took (it was reported) over £700, together with other valuables. 'Aye,' Turpin is quoted as saying, 'this is the thing! That's your sort for the rag, if it would but last.'

A share of £700, considering the value of the pound in those days, was bigger money than Turpin was accustomed to. It was more profitable than cattle-stealing and no more dangerous; and if the thought of honest farm-labouring had ever entered the head of the rough tough Turpin at the age of thirty it was now and for ever to be dismissed. In farm or factory throughout the kingdom the wages of men for honest work was for the most part, according to skill, from 1s. to 2s. 6d. per day (for women, from 4d. to 1s.) and life on that could be supported, for bread cost $1\frac{1}{4}d.$ a pound, and a pound of meat (this was one of Dick Turpin's original troubles) at best fetched no more than 3d. But Turpin wished for more than marginal existence. It is not known what it would have cost to 'Bung our Eyes in Drink', but our authors suggest that Turpin was so enthusiastic about the process, and after the Rippleside adventure was so well heeled for a prolonged spree, as to cause him to miss the next outing. However, there were others:

London Evening Post, Thursday, February 6, 1735.
February 4th. On Tuesday night, about Eight o'Clock, five Villains came to the house of Mr Lawrence, a Farmer at Edgewarebury, near Edgeware, in Middlesex, but the Door being bolted, they could not get in, so they went to the Boy who was in the Sheep-house, and compell'd him to call the Maid, who open'd the Door, upon which they rush'd in, bound the Master, Maid, and one Man-servant, and swore they would murder all the Family if they did not discover their Money &c. they trod the bedding under foot, in case there should be money hidden in it, and took about 10£ in money, Linnen &c. all they could lay Hands on, broke the Old Man's Head, dragg'd him about the House, emptied a kettle of water from the fire over him, which had fortunately only just been placed on it, and ravish'd the Maid, Dorothy Street, using her in a most barbarious Manner, they went off, leaving the Family bound. . . .

A further item appeared a few days later:

London Evening Post, Tuesday, February 11, 1735.
Mr Lawrence, the Farmer at Edgeware-bury who was robb'd last Week (as we mention'd) lies so ill, of the Bruises &c. he

receiv'd that it is question'd whether he will recover, the Rogues, after he had told them where his Money was, not finding so much as they expected, let his Breeches down, and sat him bare on the fire, three several times, which burnt him prodigiously.

There had been many similar episodes in which the loot had been disappointing and in which the Gang had violently vented such disappointment. This episode was the last. With what seems very commendable speed the constables picked up various members, as reported in the *London Gazette*, 18 February to 22 February 1735: namely John Wheeler, who was committed to New Prison, and turned informer on the others, who were Joseph Rose, Humphrey Walker, John Palmer, and William Saunders. There was a mistake, I think, about this 'John Palmer' who existed only as an alias; but the others were caught and dumped in Newgate. Also Joseph Gregory, brother of the gang-leader, was put into Chelmsford Gaol; and Mary Johnson, alias Brazier, alias Rose, was committed to the Gate-house, Westminster, as being accessory in receiving the goods, knowing them to be stolen. But the *London Gazette* admits that four of the most important of the Gang are still wanted, for whom it repeats the offer of substantial reward:

> The Persons undermentioned are charged upon Oath for committing several Robberies in Essex, Middlesex, Surrey and Kent, and are not yet taken, for each of whom a Reward of Fifty Pounds is advertized in the *Gazettes* of the 4th and 7th of January last past and on the 8th and 11th of this instant February.
> Samuel Gregory, lodged lately at Joseph Gregory's his Brother's a Carman in Old Gravel Lane, Radcliff. He is about five feet seven inches High, has a Scar about an Inch and a Half Long on his Right Cheek, is fresh coloured wears a Brown Wig and about 23 years old is a Smith or Farrier by Trade.
> Thomas Rowden lately arrived at Radcliff Highway towards the lower end of Shadwell Church, is a little man, well set, fresh coloured and full faced, has small Pockholes in his Face, wears a Blue Grey Coat and a Light Wig, a Pewterer by Trade, aged about 30 years.
> Herbert Haines, a Barber or Perriwig Maker by Trade Kept a Barber's Shop in Hog Lane in Shoreditch he is about five feet seven inches High, of a Pale Complexion, wears a Brown Wig and a Brick Coloured Cloth Coat, aged about 24 years.
> Richard Turpin, a Butcher by Trade, is a Tall Fresh Coloured

little. We saw that Rowden the Pewterer considered road-work a mug's game and preferred counterfeiting. What we have to contemplate is what Turpin acquired in hard cash as a highwayman, even with so talented a partner as King.

Before, and long after Turpin's time, there was much play in the newspapers about highwaymen because, I was suggesting, it was saleable news-matter. *The Beggar's Opera* by John Gay, first produced in 1728, had done something to make highwaymen a romantic subject; so had Defoe's *Moll Flanders*, dated 1721. Much later, on Boswell's first journey to London in 1762, it will be remembered that in spite of having armed himself he 'was a good deal afraid of robbers'. Boswell had read about them. But I don't recall that in his gaddings about Boswell was ever actually molested, and there is a good general test to be applied as to the amount of truth the public really accorded to the appre-hensions played on by newspapers. Was the risk of robbery such as to induce people to take out insurance? Marine insurance, fire insurance, life insurance had been matters of general importance in England for a very long time. So far as I can find out, Mr William Waller of Welbeck Street was the first to endeavour, in 1787, to found an insurance company for the protection of property against burglary, robbery, or activity of footpads. Mr Waller's endeavour failed. There did not seem to be enough apprehension of risk. (Burglary insurance as we now know it came into being in 1889.)

Nor, despite the excitement for the highwayman and the perpetual hope that the next strike might be a bigger one, and despite such glory as there might be at being at the top of their profession, were Turpin or King deluded as to the amounts of their takings. Unguarded road-travellers simply did not carry vast bags of gold. An occasional take was £40; more often £6, or £4, or 15s., or nothing. The hide-out of theirs in Epping Forest (when discovered it was only supposed to be theirs because nobody else ever claimed it) was a cavern within a thicket 'wherein was a Bed of Hay, part of a Loaf, part of a Bottle of Wine, and three clean Shirts'. Their putting up at an inn was often risky. They both understood very well the points of a horse, and despite all the newspaper items about robbery from the person, the more reliable income for Turpin and King came from horse-stealing and horse-trading. A snag was to steal horses which were good enough to sell but unidentifiable. In April 1737 Turpin and King stole a bay mare, unfortunately a steeple-chaser with a known name, White Stockings. Bob King's brother Matthew comes momentarily into the picture as being commissioned to hide White Stockings at an inn in Whitechapel; but the horse was identified, and when Bob King and Turpin came to claim it Matthew was in the hands of the innkeeper and a constable. There are many versions of the fracas, but the truth would seem to be that Bob King went ahead on foot to get the horse, while Turpin, mounted, was in the background. The quarrel was instant: Bob King shot at the innkeeper, but missed, and the innkeeper shot Bob King mortally; and Turpin, riding in, with a hasty shot hit, by mistake, Matthew. There was nothing for Turpin to do but ride off, his best friend gone, and when he had ridden back to the Epping Forest cavern-in-a-thicket with the 'Bed of Hay, part of a Loaf, part of a Bottle of Wine, and three clean Shirts', it must all have looked empty.

It is noticeable in Turpin's character that immediately after a setback his temper was apt to be ungovernable. He was nursing revenge upon Mr Bayes, of the Green Man in Epping Forest, whom he considered responsible for the identification of White Stockings and the death of Bob King, when one of the underkeepers of Epping Forest approached too close to Dick's hide-out. The underkeeper was accompanied by 'a Higgler'. I understand a higgler to be a small trader who took country produce to town and on return brought shop goods. It was on 4 May that the underkeeper approached too close and Turpin 'shot him in the Belly Dead on the Spot'. The higgler ran away.

Thereafter, starting in June and continuing for several weeks, newspapers printed the proclamation that there was now a reward of £200 for information leading to Turpin's arrest. Description, such as might have applied to a good many men on horseback, was appended. A lot of people were seen, riding hither or thither, at places far apart. That, I believe, was what brought into the legend of Turpin his miraculous mare, Black Bess.

Not brought into the legend, but possibly to be brought into the character-sketch, is the item that in the June and July of 1737 'Rowden the Pewterer', apprehended under an assumed name at Gloucester for counterfeiting, had been identified, tried at Chelmsford for having been a highwayman, then 'brought back to Newgate with his legs chained under a Horse's Belly' for further trial for the old Middlesex robberies.

Exit Rowden. Of the old Gang, Turpin was the only one left. But it is my guess that even before he might have heard of Rowden, Turpin had ceased to be. That is to say, he vanished from the area in which newspapers continued to accuse him of operating. Doubtless other highwaymen were at work, and throughout the summer of 1737 every hold-up was blamed upon the legendary Turpin, most interesting of spectres now that he carried £200 reward. A name well planted in the consciousness, Dick Turpin. In the meantime there turned up inconspicuously at Long Sutton in Lincolnshire a stranger from the south who called himself John Palmer. I think this may have been a previous alias of Turpin's in earlier days with Gregory's Gang; it was an alias not difficult to invent, for Turpin's father's name was John, and his mother's name had been Palmer; perhaps for that reason not a very good alias, but it served in Lincolnshire. John Palmer was not questioned at Long Sutton, until there happened to be complaints of sheep-stealing. John Palmer was suspected, a warrant was issued and served by a constable; but John Palmer knocked down the constable and departed from that district.

Palmer was adept at acquiring and selling horses, and while innkeepers in the Home Counties were furbishing up and showing authentic relics of the famous Turpin, the beds he slept in and the coats he left behind him in his quick escapes, and while the spate of reports about Turpin was still in the news, the man Palmer was drifting slowly northward until he came to Brough, near Market Cave in Yorkshire, Palmer continued to be in that neighbourhood until October 1738, although with frequent visits into Lincolnshire 'to see his Friends'. On return from these visits he would usually bring 'three or four Horses' to sell in Yorkshire. He seemed usually to have enough money to spend and in Brough he rubbed along without much question. It is said that he made friends with a married woman in Brough, but about that there is no more to be known than that in the final dispersal of his possessions he left to her a gold ring, two pairs of shoes, and clogs.

The name of Turpin, having been run in the newspapers
in 1737 for as much as it was worth, for more than a year
dropped out completely. It returned to the Press in an odd
little item:

Worcester Journal, September 29, 1738.
A few days since the father of the noted Turpin was committed to Chelmsford Gaol, for having in his possession a
Horse, supposed to be stolen out of Lincolnshire, which he
pleads, was left with him by his son for Diet and Lodging.

By curious coincidence it was on an afternoon early in
October that John Palmer in Yorkshire gave a singular
display of bad temper. He had been out shooting, with
no luck. On return, one of his landlord's cockerels appeared
in front of him in the town street. Palmer shot and killed it.
A neighbour, Mr Hall, immediately remonstrated: 'Mr
Palmer, you have done wrong in shooting your landlord's
cock'—to which Palmer replied that 'if he would only stay
while he charged his piece he would shoot him, too'. The
incensed Mr Hall told the landlord, the landlord told the
constable, complaint was lodged, warrant obtained, and
on 3 October John Palmer was arrested to go before the
magistrate, Mr Cowle, at Beverley Petty Sessions. Antici-
pating nothing more serious than an accusation of wanton
mischief when drunk, Palmer went along quietly to Beverley.
It was careless of him to ride to Beverley upon a black
gelding which was later proved to have been stolen.
As to the quarrel about the shooting of the cockerel, all
that Mr Cowle ordered was that Palmer should find sureties
for future good behaviour. This was unexpectedly difficult
for Palmer, who had no influential friends and no antecedents.
Under question, where had he come from, Palmer mentioned
Long Sutton. Mr Cowle pursued the matter with a letter to
Long Sutton, and Long Sutton replied that all that was
known about him there was the warrant against him for
sheep-stealing, with strong suspicions of horse-stealing. This
reply caused Palmer to be removed in custody from Beverley
to York Castle. Evidence about horses which he had stolen
(including the black gelding) was quickly to be obtained,
and Palmer was worried enough to write to his brother-in-
law at Hempstead. His hope was that if he could obtain 'a

character' he might possibly achieve a sentence of transportation rather than hanging.

It was very awkward for Palmer that John Turpin of Hempstead was in Chelmsford Gaol for a horse 'supposed to be stolen out of Lincolnshire' and 'left with him by his son', for Hempstead was bound to be agog about this. But Palmer thought it safe to write to his brother-in-law in a veiled way. 'Dear Brother' was asked to procure somehow 'a character' for 'you will know what I mean when I say . . . John Palmer'. Now the fatal accident happened. For some reason the letter from York was not accepted at the address given and was returned to the Hempstead postmaster; for some reason the postmaster showed the envelope to Mr Smith, the schoolmaster who had taught Richard Turpin to write. Mr Smith thought he recognized the handwriting; he was in fact so sure (the guess might be worth £200) that he took the envelope to a magistrate; the letter was officially opened, and manifestly John Palmer and Richard Turpin were one and the same. For confirmation Mr Smith was sent to York, the prisoners at the Castle were paraded; Mr Smith picked out Turpin at once, and Turpin acknowledged with the phrase: 'Let us Bung our Eyes in Drink.'

The trial took place at York Assizes on 22 March 1739. The verbatim record indicates that the judge, Sir William Chapple, was efficient and fair. The defendant had nothing whatever to say. The verdict was guilty and the sentence was death. Dick Turpin was hanged on 7 April at The Mount, just outside Micklegate Bar, York.

The legend, created I think by newspapers, led to various ballads (none that I have seen is very good) and to the preposterous romantic writing of Harrison Ainsworth (*Rookwood*, 1833). There never was a ride to York by Turpin on Black Bess. If anyone comes well out of the factual story it is not the sensation-mongers: it is the cops who come out well and not the robbers. I am not sure about the informer. Just before Dick was hanged, John Turpin, the father, was released from Chelmsford, in time to write the son a farewell letter from Hempstead. It is a very pious letter, very beautifully expressed, somewhat literary, suggestive somehow that the innkeeper might have had some conscientious assistance from the village schoolmaster.

The
CABINET
of
Curiosities

The Unnatural History of the Salamander

BY
JOHN
VINDEN

THE PHOENIX and the salamander of legend have one thing in common—their ability to withstand fire with impunity. Since the phoenix was such a rare bird, opportunities for observing its habits were few and far between; yet, in spite of the fact that the salamander has always been a common animal, some of the strange legends concerning it are still believed.

The legendary salamander was a sort of lizard reputed to live in fire and be nourished by it. It was further believed that the most violent fire was extinguished when a salamander was thrown into it. When these stories were currently believed a wonderful incombustible material found its way to the West, and on account of its miraculous qualities was given the name of 'salamander's wool'.

This incombustible wool was, of course, asbestos, and its mineral origin was known quite early to those who preferred fact to fable. One of these enlightened people was Sir Thomas Browne, who wrote:

> The fable of the salamander hath been much promoted by stories of incombustible napkins and textures that endure the fire, whose materials are called by the name of Salamanders' wool, which many too literally apprehending conceive some investing part or integument of the Salamander. . . . Nor is this Salamanders' wool desumed from any animal, but a mineral substance, metaphorically so called for this received opinion.

The majority of people, both in Europe and Asia, preferred to believe that this material was derived from the salamander —a somewhat surprising fact, as the salamander is not a woolly animal.

Jerome Cardan, a sixteenth-century Italian scientist, searched in vain for hairs on the salamander, and others wondered from which part of the animal the wool was derived. An ingenious answer to this problem was that the salamander was a sort of silkworm; that the wool did not actually grow on the animal but was spun by it. Prester John is alleged to have told Manuel Comnenus, Emperor of Constantinople, that the salamander made cocoons, and that the material woven from these was impervious to fire.

Although from the time of Aristotle the salamander bore the reputation of being fireproof, its wool was not mentioned till a much later date. The belief in the wool, however, was well established by the thirteenth century, when Marco Polo thought it necessary to contradict this story.

> . . . in the same mountain there is a vein of the substance from which salamander is made. For the real truth is that the Salamander is no beast, but is a substance found in the earth.

M

He goes on to tell us how the raw material was treated, and how the finished asbestos could be woven into cloth which would withstand the action of fire.

There must at one time have been a not inconsiderable trade in such novelties as asbestos cloth, which is, after all, a rather wonderful material. Its connection with the salamander would, no doubt, have grown from the legends already current about this amphibian.

Today this rather engaging beast, the European salamander, has no habits or venomous ways that render it dangerous to man. But this was not always so—according to legend. Pliny tells us that

> He is of so cold a complexion, that if he do but touch fire, he will quench it as presently as if ice were put into it. The Salamander casteth up at the mouth a certain venomous matter like milk, let it but once touch any bare part of a man or woman's body, all their hair will fall off, and the part so touched will change the colour of the skin to a white morphew.

Not only was the salamander credited with the ability to extinguish fire but it was given more sinister attributes. Salamanders today can be handled with impunity and the skin retains its original colour, but Pliny did not let the poor beast rest, for he also stated that

> . . . the salamander is able to destroy whole nations at one time, if they take not heed and provide to prevent them; for if he once gets to a tree, and either clasp about it or creep upon it, all the fruit that it bears is infected with his venom, and sure they are to die; whosoever eat of that fruit . . . or if one of them chance to fall into a well or pit of water, look whosoever drink thereof, shall be sure to die upon it.

Pliny told us that if the salamander touched a piece of wood with which a loaf is baked or a piece of bread toasted the consumer of the bread would be poisoned. We have in this story some fascinating speculations. Illness following the eating of bread (or toast for that matter) can usually be traced to rye-flour poisoned with ergot, and in the past many such epidemics have been recorded. In A.D. 922 it is said that no fewer than forty thousand people died from eating ergotized bread in France alone, and in 1128–9 in Paris fourteen thousand people died of 'Ignis Sacer' or gangrenous

174

ergotism. As recently as 1951 there was an outbreak of a similar kind in France involving two hundred people.

A disease like this could not be explained in the days of Pliny, and such occurrences were either attributed to divine intervention or blamed on to some harmless creature. When the outbreak began somebody would remember seeing a salamander near the scene; they would apply the muddled reasoning of *post hoc ergo propter hoc*, and so a new legend would be born.

Water-borne diseases like typhoid fever and cholera were caused not by our salamander in the well but by lack of sanitation. At certain seasons of the year salamanders enter the water; therefore, by the same argument, they were responsible for the outbreaks of disease.

The salamander's capacity for wholesale poisoning was believed for a very long time, for Glanvil, an English writer of the thirteenth century, states as an historic fact that four thousand men and two thousand horses of Alexander the Great's army were killed through drinking from a stream contaminated by salamanders.

The salamander enjoyed his unenviable reputation for a long, long time, but in the delightful medieval bestiaries the salamander is portrayed as a symbol of the Christian who has passed unscathed through the fires of passion. It consequently acquired a virtuous reputation for the first time.

Our first problem is, how did the salamander come to acquire its reputation of being fireproof? The real salamander, although bearing a superficial resemblance to a lizard, is really an amphibian, as are frogs and newts. Instead of having dry scales like a lizard, it has a damp, cold, and clammy skin.

Touch a salamander: it feels cold. Moreover, it looks a little like a fire itself, with its skin black like coal and yellow markings bright like flames. With some stretch of imagination the animal can be said to be fire-like. We know that, in the past, many people believed that 'like cured like'; consequently, a flame-like animal would extinguish flames.

The belief in the incombustibility of the salamander lingered on, and if we are to believe our older writers the salamanders of the past *were* fireproof. In the year 1505 Benvenuto Cellini, the artist and silversmith, and, dare we say, braggart, tells us:

When I was about five years old, my father being in our small cellar, in which they had been washing the clothes, and where there was still a good fire of oak boughs, Giovanni, with his viol in his arms, played and sang to himself beside that fire. By chance he saw in the midst of the hottest flames a little animal like a lizard, which was sporting about amidst the most scorching blaze. Having immediately perceived what it was he caused my sister and me to be summoned, and pointing it to us children, he gave me a violent box on the ear, at which I began to cry most excessively. He comforting me kindly, spake to me thus: 'My dear little son, I did not give you that blow on account of anything wrong you have done, but only that you may remember that that lizard that you saw in the fire is a salamander, a creature that has never been seen by anyone else of whom we have reliable information.'

One would, like father Cellini, be inclined to suggest that this incident was unique in the annals of natural history were it not for the fact that so distinguished a person as the editor of the *Philosophical Transactions of the Royal Society* saw fit to publish the following in 1716:

A salamander on being thrown into the fire the animal thereupon swelled presently and then vomited store of thick slimy matter, which did put out the neighbouring Coals, to which the salamander retired immediately, putting them out again in the same manner, as soon as they rekindled; and by this means saving himself from the force of the fire for the space of two hours; That afterwards it lived for nine months.

This is a very circumstantial story indeed, but we must cast some doubt upon it, for in 1742 some further experiments were carried out on the salamander by the Rev. Charles Owen, who leaves us the following report:

The Salamander is of a poisonous nature, and many have suffered from its biting; so says Pliny, with whom agree Nicander, Aetius, and Abensinae. Gesner is of a contrary sentiment, and says he had domestic salamanders, that offered no violence with their teeth without provocation. Johnstonus adds, that in Germany there appeared no ill effects of its bite, but in France its wounds were of a most deadly nature, as appears by a saying in that kingdom namely 'that a man bit by a salamander should have as many physicians to cure him, as the salamander has spots' which are numerous. The common report is that the salamander is able to live in the fire, which is a vulgar error. The Hieroglyphicle Historian observes, that upon trial made, it was so far from quenching it that it consumed immediately.

So we see that the salamander can be consumed by fire after all, and that at that period the belief in its venomous qualities was limited to certain countries.

Notwithstanding its alleged preference for fire, the real salamander is said to recover after being frozen solidly in ice, thus showing that it can enjoy a very wide range of temperature.

Error has piled upon error as far as the salamander is concerned, and it is interesting to note that a salamander, but not our little fire-loving species, was the cause of much general excitement in the early eighteenth century. Today in Japan and China there are giant salamanders, and there were at one time other such giant species, now long extinct. In 1726 the fossil skeleton of a giant species was discovered at Basle by the scientist Scheuchzer, who named it *Homo diluvii testis*, that is to say, 'man a witness of the flood'. The discoverer believed it to be a human skeleton which had been buried as a result of Noah's deluge. This may seem an unpardonable error, but we must remember that these were the early days of palaeontology. Even today it is not always easy to assign stray fossils to their rightful position in the scheme of things, and in spite of all modern aids it took specialists many years to settle, finally, the arguments concerning the now notorious Piltdown skull.

There was a certain romance connected with the discovery of the living giant salamanders. They were discovered by Seibold in the rivers of Japan, but his first specimen was bought by him in a food market where it was being offered as a delicacy. He brought two living specimens to Europe in 1829, one of which survived until 1881.

Is there any modern counterpart to the salamander of legend? There is, alas, no incombustible lizard in the world today, and the only place where this animal exists in flames is in heraldry, for François I of France had as his badge 'a lizard in the midst of flames' with the legend *Nutrisco et extinguo* (I nourish and extinguish).

There are, however, certain animals that can endure unusually high temperatures, none of them a salamander.

Since various temperatures are to be mentioned, it should

be pointed out that all the figures cited are Fahrenheit. Although this scale is not that adopted by modern science, it is that with which we are most familiar.

Most animals are fairly conservative about the temperature in which they live, and extremes of temperature in either direction rapidly prove fatal to the vast majority of lower organisms. There is, for instance, a little aquatic creature, a flatworm, *Crenobia alpina*, which occurs in parts of Europe in cold streams formed by melting ice and snow. During the Ice Age this little worm would have flourished all over Europe, but as the ice withdrew from the more temperate parts of the continent the animal became locally extinct because it could not tolerate the higher temperatures.

This relic of the Ice Age has survived in Britain in the mountainous parts of Scotland, Wales, and the Lake District and also in isolated low-lying streams where the temperature never exceeds 60 degrees. Temperatures above this are fatal to the animal. This creature always moves upstream to lay its eggs, for the higher it goes, the colder the water.

At the other extreme are those animals that live in hot springs. Although the population of hot springs is not a very varied one, some of the higher animals exist in such springs under conditions which appear to be unfavourable to animal life. Aquatic creatures that do not breathe atmospheric air have to rely on oxygen dissolved in the water in which they live, and although cold water is capable of holding a fair amount of dissolved oxygen, the warmer the water becomes the less the quantity of oxygen present.

Pure water at 50 degrees is capable of absorbing nearly eight parts per thousand, by volume, of oxygen, whereas warm water of 90 degrees can absorb only five parts per thousand. It can be seen, therefore, that the difficulty of obtaining oxygen must be very great in waters of high temperature. In spite of this, a fish, *Barbus callensis*, that is common in Algeria, and has also been recorded in southern Europe, has been found in hot springs living in water with the astonishing temperature of 180 degrees. At this temperature it would be possible to cook an egg!

In many of these cases, however, there is a sharp temperature gradient. Hot water rises and cold water sinks, so that the temperature in which the animal actually lives may not be as hot as would appear from a casual measurement with an ordinary thermometer. In some deserts there are many animals capable of enduring high temperatures for short periods, and insects can be seen at rest on the surface of deserts at temperatures as high as 145 degrees. Many of these are protected from the surface heat by their long legs which hold their bodies away from the ground.

This temperature would be fatal to most species of insects, although one beetle, *Trogoderma granarium*, which attacks stored grain, will feed on malt at a temperature of 120 degrees, and the fire brat, *Thermobia domestica*, of Europe and America, lives like the salamander of legend in the vicinity of furnaces. In the other direction is the insect *Grylloblatta* which can be kept alive only on ice.

During the 1914–18 War it was frequently found that sealed tins of army biscuits were infested with insect life. Entomologists were called in to try to discover when the infection took place and experiments were carried out to find at what temperature the insects and their eggs were destroyed, and also whether the entire biscuit reached this temperature during the process of baking.

It was discovered that a temperature of 126·1 degrees for twelve minutes killed the eggs of the flour moth, and that a temperature of 132·4 degrees coagulated the albumen in all insect eggs and, therefore, destroyed them. Since the biscuits were known to reach higher temperatures than these during the process of baking, it was realized that the infection must have taken place between baking and the sealing of the tins.

However, the eggs of insects can often survive higher temperatures than the insects themselves or their larvae.

It will be seen from such results that even odd bits of natural history lore can have profound practical results.

Hitherto we have dealt with 'cold-blooded' as opposed to 'warm-blooded' animals such as birds and mammals. Both these terms are, in fact, misnomers, and better, if more clumsy, terms in English would be 'changeable temperature' and 'constant temperature' animals. The so-called cold-blooded creatures can be quite warm-blooded if they are in warm surroundings, and the warm-blooded animals may, on occasion, have blood somewhat cooler than their environment.

The warm-blooded or constant-temperature animals, however, usually have blood considerably warmer than their surroundings. For instance, the average July temperature in England is around 66 degrees, man's temperature is normally 98·6 degrees, and that of the average bird around 106 degrees.

Maintenance of a constant temperature in the body is quite a problem for a warm-blooded animal and the task varies according to the animal and its environment.

How does man compare with the salamander for temperature survival? What temperatures can he endure? Under what conditions can he endure them? Apart from the standards of the thermometer we have no yardstick to decide what is hot and what is cold. While the physicist can talk about such temperatures as absolute zero, the layman can think only in terms within his experience. Most of us are familiar with ice, but few can imagine the sensation of touching something, say, four times colder than ice.

To the ordinary person a 'hot' cup of tea is a very hot one at 160 degrees, though naturally individuals differ over such comparisons. Man can work in the boiler-rooms of ships in the tropics at temperatures exceeding 150 degrees provided that the atmosphere is dry and that he has brackish water to drink to replace the salt and water lost in perspiration.

Joseph Banks, the great naturalist and traveller, remained for some time in a room at a temperature of 211 degrees, but his internal body temperature did not rise at all.

We all have personal views on what is hot and what is cold. Some enjoy a brisk walk on a frosty morning; others would rather stay in bed. The terms 'hot' and 'cold' are, of course, purely relative, and it is staggering how we use these words without considering their meaning. On a spring morning we complain that at 38 degrees it is cold. At lunch-time a waiter brings soup at a temperature of 110 degrees and again we complain that it is 'cold'. With lunch we have a glass of lager beer served at about 45 degrees, and complain that it is warm. So it goes on; hot and cold, cold and hot.

There are times, of course, when we *are* hot. When we have fever and a higher-than-normal temperature. Temperatures such as these, though only a few degrees higher than normal, are considered to be dangerous. Temperatures in fever as high as 108 degrees are rare and are not often survived, yet in 1895, at a meeting of the Association of

Signora Josephine Giraldelli, the Original Salamander, 1819

American Physicians, Dr Jacobi of New York reported a case of a man whose temperature reached the astounding figure of 148 degrees. This man, who appropriately enough happened to be a fireman, is said to have maintained a temperature averaging 122 degrees for five days.

Early in the last century there was exhibited at Bartholomew Fair the 'Fireproof Lady', one Mme Giraldelli. It was said that she could bear the heat of the furnace with impunity.

She put melted lead into her mouth and spat it out marked with her teeth. She would pass red-hot irons over her body and limbs, her tongue, and her hair. She would thrust her hand and arms into the fire and wash her hands, not only in boiling lead, but in *aqua fortis* as well. This, as one can see, must have been a very impressive performance indeed, and, no doubt, trickery contributed to her success.

Wood's metal, an alloy that melts at a temperature of approximately 155 degrees, could have been substituted for lead. It would still, admittedly, be unpleasantly hot in the mouth, but not fatal, and great artists often suffer in the cause of their art. The passing of red-hot irons *near* the skin, provided that it is done quickly, requires but dexterity and confidence, but washing the hands in boiling oil and nitric acid is a practice not to be recommended.

Chamouni, the 'Russian Salamander', who, as was afterwards proved, rashly assumed the title 'The Incombustible', was the subject of an article in *The Lancet* in 1828. This article, or shall we say obituary notice, went as follows:

> The Russian Salamander was remarkable for the simplicity and singleness of his character, as well as for that idiosyncrasy of his constitution, which enabled him, for so many years, not merely to brave the effects of fire, but to take delight in an element where other men find destruction. He was above all artifice, and would often entreat his visitors to melt their own lead, or boil their own mercury, that they might be properly satisfied of the gratification he derived from drinking these preparations. He would also present his tongue, in the most obliging manner, to all who wished to pour melted lead upon it, and stamp an impression of their seals. His merit, however, was never sufficiently acknowledged till he was found dead in the oven which he had so often entered to amuse his visitors, but what he called his grand experiment was to enter an oven with a raw leg of mutton, and not to retire from it till the joint was thoroughly baked. Chamouni entered this oven once too often; his ashes were collected, and conveyed to Mojaisk, his native town, where a neat monument has been erected to his memory, and a well-written Latin inscription commemorates his fate.

The race of human salamanders is not yet extinct, for on 26 September 1952 it was reported in *The Times* that a fire-eater at Hastings crouched in a metal box in the midst of a fire said to be about 3,000 degrees. Although it was advertised as a 'cremation', this gentleman came out from his crucible none the worse for his experience.

The fire-walkers of the East and the Navajo Indians of America, who practise fire-worship and handle fire with impunity, have been the subject of speculation for centuries. Some held that they were under the influence of drugs or hypnotism, others that they treated their feet with chemicals.

Nobody, apparently, made any serious investigation of this odd phenomenon until 1934, when that enthusiastic investigator of the unknown, the late Harry Price, started making enquiries and began a series of controlled experiments both with professional Indian fire-walkers and with British volunteers. The results of these experiments were astounding in many ways. It was discovered that no trickery was involved, and that no preparation of the feet was necessary.

At the final test, which was televised from the grounds of Alexandra Palace in London on 20 April 1937, the surface temperature of the fire was 1,472 degrees. This temperature, translated into homely terms, is roughly seven times that of boiling water. An Indian and an English volunteer both walked this fire without coming to harm.

The secret of fire-walking apparently lies in the fact that the actual time of contact with the burning embers is momentary, and also that the feet must be perfectly dry. All the walkers were burnt if more than four steps were taken.

Modern performers in the circus ring and on the stage run flaming torches up and down their limbs without apparent discomfort. They also 'eat' fire. The fire in this case usually consists of highly inflammable vapour which ignites readily when exhaled. It is a dangerous occupation at the best, and a sudden fit of coughing could lead to highly unpleasant results.

During the Suez Crisis of 1957, when petrol was rationed in England, it was reported that a nineteen-year-old fire-eater, whose professional name was Zahrat, was granted a ration of petrol to enable her to continue her performances. For official purposes, the regional petroleum officer listed her as a 'stationary plant'.

It can be seen that, in spite of the salamander of legend, man, with no more equipment than that with which nature provided him, can endure temperatures far greater than any other animal.

The Men who were Never Alone

BY CLIVE BEECH

NOWADAYS, ALL identical twins who have the misfortune to be born joined together are described, both scientifically and popularly, as Siamese twins, and doctors are becoming increasingly successful at separating them as babies. But what of the original Siamese Twins, who lent their name to this condition of multiple birth? They gave a new expression to the language, yet their story has been rarely told.

They were not, as is generally supposed, the first otherwise normal human beings to be born and live joined together. Similar though distinctly rare cases had been known for many centuries earlier, the most famous probably being Eliza and Mary Chulkhurst, the Biddenden Maids, who were born in 1100 in the little village of Biddenden in Kent, joined at the hips and shoulders, and lived there to the age of thirty-four, doing good works and founding the charity which is still bestowed annually among the poor. But the Siamese Twins were the first joined twins to become widely known outside their native land.

They were not in fact pure Siamese. They were born in the little village of Meklong, on the Siam River near Bangkok, and they spent their early youth in Siam. Their father, however, was Chinese, an impoverished fisherman, and their mother was a poor Siamese peasant woman who produced other quite normal offspring. She named her freak twins Chang and Eng.

At birth they were found to be joined together at the breast-bone by a cartilaginous band. This thick, fleshy ligament covered with skin, rather like a four-inch-long arm, linked them firmly down as far as their lower chests. Otherwise they were completely normally formed human beings.

At first their band held them face to face, but as the babies grew it began to stretch slightly, finally reaching a length of about five and a half inches. This enabled them to move

184

sideways, and to stand more or less normally, with only a slight outward tilt. The joining band that made them so different from everyone else in the world was tough yet elastic, allowing considerable freedom of movement yet always limiting their freedom. If an outsider touched it exactly in the centre both boys received the sensation. If one of them tripped or lost his balance the mutual ligament prevented him from falling, leaving him dangling from his brother, but firmly held.

As humble Siamese children, the Twins mastered the basic difficulties of living joined together, and, after early trials, managed to walk and run in step. They also learned to swim well together when quite young, which odd faculty probably changed the whole course of their lives. Although they were favourite guests at the fabulous Royal Palace in Bangkok (the setting of *The King and I*), they lived remarkably normal lives until 1830, when they were nineteen years old. They still regularly disported themselves in the river, and in that year were seen swimming by a visiting American sea-captain, Captain Coffin, master of the *Sachem*. Agog with what he saw, he told a shrewd Scots trader named Robert Hunter, and together they decided to try to purchase the lads and exhibit them for the financial gain they believed would be readily forthcoming in Europe. It was to prove a wise, if unorthodox, speculation.

It so happened that the boys' father had lately died, and their mother preferred the offered cash to their company. A deal was swiftly done, and Coffin and Hunter took Chang and Eng to England. The strange pair were regularly shown on the Continent for many years, exciting curiosity, horror, indignation, disbelief. Their sponsors made a lot of money in an age of simple credulity and sensation-seeking, undeterred when pompous folk wrote letters to the newspapers protesting that such an exhibition would deprave the minds of children, or when France refused them entry since the authorities there believed that any expectant mother who saw them might give birth to similar freaks.

Medically speaking, Siamese twins are twins produced from incompletely split eggs. They are always identical twins, and thus of the same sex, and varying degrees of fusion, or rather lack of separation, are known. Extreme cases usually perish at birth, but in the case of Chang and

Eng the linkage was only at one point of the body, which explains why they survived.

Nevertheless, Fate played the cruellest of tricks upon them. So close physically, they were poles apart in every other way. Chang was the shifty-looking, slightly shorter brother on the Twins' own left. He was wayward, indolent, irascible, overfond of drink and women. His brother, on his right side, was quiet, studious, calm, sober, and much more intellectual. Eng liked nothing better than a quiet evening of chess. As the *Medical Times*, Philadelphia, put it in 1874:

> What Chang liked to eat, Eng detested. Eng was very good-natured, Chang cross and irritable. The sickness of one had no effect upon the other, so that while one would be suffering from fever, the pulse of the other would beat at its natural rate. Chang drank pretty heavily—at times getting drunk; but Eng never felt any influence from the debauch of the brother. They often quarrelled; and, of course, under the circumstances their quarrels were bitter. They sometimes came to blows, and on one occasion came under the jurisdiction of the courts.

Thus diametrically opposed, they hated each other all their lives, embodying in one combined frame the schizophrenia found in all of us. When left alone they would sit brooding in melancholy silence. At times they would agree to do first what one brother wanted, then what the other wanted; but arguments were continual. The only mutual interests they possessed in adult life were cutting firewood, fishing, and hunting. Steady compromise of action seemed to elude them. Yet both were intelligent men.

After one really bad quarrel they decided they must be parted or go mad. They had already consulted innumerable doctors, qualified and otherwise, on this possibility that had always been uppermost in both their minds. But always the verdict was the same: no surgeon could guarantee their survival if they were cut apart. This time they went to their own doctor, Dr Hollingsworth, and demanded to be separated. Eng claimed that Chang was so bad that he could no longer live with him. Chang asked only that he be given an equal chance with his brother, and that their connecting band be severed exactly in the middle. In the end, however, both Twins were made to see cool reason, and in spite of all the arguments and all the consultations in both Europe and America, no such operation on them was ever attempted.

Coffin and Hunter decided to try to repeat their European successes in America, and showed the Twins first at Boston, where they became known, unhappily, as The Monster, and thence to New York and other cities, where they were advertised as The Siamese Double Boys.

A rumour spread through America that they were fakes, a pair of ordinary twins not really joined together. This controversy attracted the great Phineas T. Barnum. He met the Twins privately, questioned them, arranged for them to be medically examined, and, when convinced that they were genuine freaks, he decided that he ought to be reaping the rewards they were bringing their discoverers. He bought up their contracts, took over their sole management, and exhibited them for many years in his great American museum of oddities and curiosities at the corner of Lower Broadway and Ann Street, along with General Tom Thumb, the Fee-Jee Mermaid, and the rest. Although they were successful before Barnum had ever heard of them, it was thanks to him that they became world famous.

At this point in their careers appeared the solitary point of agreement between Chang and Eng: they both detested the great showman, felt him to be terribly stingy, and avoided him whenever they could. Nevertheless, under his banner they amassed considerable fortunes. Finally they decided to retire from the gaudy world of the sideshow and the daily sea of gaping faces. They gave Barnum notice, and planned a leisurely withdrawal from the glare of publicity.

First, however, since it was American freedom and American dollars that had enabled them to contemplate such a course whilst still in their early thirties, they decided to become American citizens. Lacking the necessary family name, they assumed that of another applicant in the line at the naturalization office who had offered it to them. Thus they became Chang and Eng Bunker, citizens of the U.S.A.

The Twins built themselves a handsome mansion on a plantation near Mount Airy, in North Carolina, settled down in the small pioneer community there, and relaxed. Slaves did all the work. It was a fitting climax to a strange and unenviable career. Only one thing was lacking. The Twins were still bachelors.

Then, when they were thirty-two years old, they met and almost simultaneously fell in love with the two virtuous daughters of a poor Irish immigrant farmer living near by. One day the Twins drove into Mount Airy's main street in their buggy, each with an arm round one of the girls, Sarah and Adelaide Yates. That was the first the neighbourhood knew of the romance. Immediately tongues began to wag and venom to flow. There was still a considerable body of public opinion that Chang and Eng were not fit to be called human; but so long as they stayed on their own plantation, that was all right. Marriage with normal girls—that was too much for public opinion to swallow! Windows were smashed at the Yates farmstead, and the girls' father was threatened with crop-burning if he allowed the association to continue. So the affair was broken up, and the unhappy pair closeted themselves back at their plantation.

True love does not recognize freaks, however, and soon the four were meeting secretly by a small bridge over a stream in the hills behind the town. This clandestine romance continued for some months, and eventually the couples decided to marry—in the face of the world's disapproval. Eng became betrothed to Sally, Chang to Addie.

But first they all agreed upon separation, so that the brothers could lead normal lives. Chang and Eng went to the College of Surgeons in Philadelphia, where they knew were eminent doctors ready to operate in the interests of science—if the pair were willing to take the terrible risk. The brothers agreed to a date, knowing full well that it might be their execution day.

On the appointed day they presented themselves to the surgeons, but, as preparations were actually going on for the severance, the two girls arrived. There was a strange and stormy scene, with tears and pleadings and arguments and protests. It ended with Chang and Eng leaving, still joined together, with their happy fiancées.

Two months later, in the spring of 1843, the little church of Mount Airy was the setting for the strangest double wedding ever seen. In spite of public shock and family dismay, the four were never in the least worried by the physical and moral complications and problems involved by their marriages. Although, inevitably, friction between the brothers continued, tact and compromise were also employed.

The Twins built another mansion, of identical size, a mile away from the first, and they speedily worked out (and religiously kept to) a plan for the establishment of two households. Eng and Sally, with Chang, spent three days and nights in Eng's home. Then Chang and Addie, with Eng, spent three days and nights at Chang's house. This odd arrangement seems to have worked perfectly. Both marriages were devoted and successful, and both wives gave their husbands large families. Sally and Eng had eleven children, Chang and Addie ten. All were sturdy and normal except two, who were born deaf and dumb. For over thirty years the twin families lived in accord.

Then came the Civil War. The Twins lost their slaves, and, in consequence, their wealth and prosperity dwindled. In the end they were forced to re-enter show business in order to live. Overcoming their dislike of Barnum—and doubtless recognizing his genius in his particular sphere—they asked him to manage them again. Unfortunately their New York comeback was a flop. Probably the war had lessened the taste of ordinary folk for horror and sensation.

Undeterred, as always, Barnum sent them to England, where they were a terrific success for about a year, Barnum having announced that the main purpose of their visit was to arrange for their severance. His special brand of hokum provided just the right fillip to jaded public interest. In actual fact, there was no truth in his announcement. Separation was never contemplated again, and there is no evidence that it was ever discussed once they had become married men with families to support.

When the Twins were over sixty they felt prosperous enough to retire for good. Their contract with Barnum was finally ended, and once more they returned to the peace and quiet of the Mount Airy plantation, Darby and Joan in duplicate, surrounded by their devoted children. Chang had been unwell for some time, but this was considered to be merely a result of his excessive drinking. The future looked happier than it had ever been. But the happiness was to be short-lived.

The end came suddenly and strangely one day in the bitter cold weather of January 1874. The *Annual Register* of the time described what happened:

They were at Chang's residence, and the evening of that day was the appointed time for a removal to Eng's dwelling. The day was cold and Chang had been complaining for a couple of months past of being very ill. On Friday evening they retired to a small room by themselves and went to bed, but Chang was very restless. Sometime between midnight and daybreak they got up and sat by the fire. Again Eng protested and said he wished to lie down as he was sleepy. Chang stoutly refused and replied that it hurt his breast to recline. After a while they retired to their bed, and Eng fell into a deep sleep. About four o'clock one of the sons came into the room, and going to the bedside, discovered that his uncle was dead. Eng was awakened by the noise and in the greatest alarm turned and looked upon the lifeless form beside him, and was seized with violent nervous paroxysms.

No physicians were at hand, and it being three miles to the town of Mount Airy, some time elapsed before one could be summoned. A messenger was despatched to the village for Dr Hollingsworth, and he sent his brother, also a physician, at once to the plantation, but before he arrived the vital spark had fled, and the Siamese Twins were dead.

Other reports of the time add that soon after realizing what had happened Eng gave a terrible cry and swiftly entered the coma with nervous spasms from which he never recovered. Clearly, before he perished Eng realized that the odious, wilful brother who had fought and thwarted him for sixty-three years was part of himself. This terrible revelation, and the discovery of being tied to a corpse, caused his own death from sheer fright.

Sally and Addie refused many offers of large sums for the purchase of their husbands' bodies, and instead they presented them to the College of Surgeons in Philadelphia. At last the doctors there were able to penetrate the riddle that had exercised them for so many years. An autopsy revealed that Chang and Eng had independent nervous systems, but that they shared a common blood-stream and liver. Separation at any time during their lives would have proved instantly fatal to both. The reason why Eng never felt the ill-effects of the large amount of alcohol taken by his brother was that Chang possessed the more sensitive of the two nervous systems and that he enjoyed less tolerance for spirits. They were two people, and yet one person.

Chang and Eng were patently meant to live together or not at all. Looking back at their strange lives, there is much to admire in the success they made of existence under perhaps the most terrible human handicap—that of never being alone.

The Joker in the Pack

BY DAVID GUNSTON

WHENEVER THE subject of practical joking crops up one name is always quoted: that of Horace de Vere Cole. With the years it has achieved classic status in the annals of the jest, alongside such immortals as Theodore Hook, of the Berners Street hoax, and Wilhelm Voigt, the notorious 'Captain of Koepenick'. With continued retelling, too, his japes have become rather heavily embroidered, though the man himself becomes ever more unreal and shadowy. As he died as long ago as 1936, and still lacks a full-length biography, the time is ripe for a reappraisal of this prince of English jesters (he was in fact Anglo-Irish) both as a man and as a *farceur*.

Just what sort of a person was Cole? How and why did he become a hoaxer extraordinary, a kind of unofficial national joker during some of the stuffiest years of our history? This necessarily brief account is an attempt to answer these questions. If, at the end, the man seems just as unreal, perhaps the reason will be that he was a true Rabelaisian, born out of his time. Anyway, his exploits always bear recounting!

William Horace de Vere Cole was born in 1881, the eldest son of Major W. N. Cole, a stalwart of the 3rd Dragoon Guards, by his marriage with the wealthy heiress Mary de Vere, who came from Issercleran, Co. Galway. Little is known of his childhood, save that it was spent in both Ireland and England. He was sent to Eton (Mr Ainger's house), and in 1900, when still only eighteen, left to fight in the Boer War, in which he distinguished himself and was severely wounded. On his return to England he went up to Trinity College, Cambridge, and from then on he seems to have dedicated his life to the serious pursuit of the practical joke. A bizarre and unprofitable role, perhaps, but one he was to fill to perfection.

Unlike most would-be wags and wits, Cole can be said to have been born to his vocation. The fates had showered upon him all the necessary attributes of the big-time hoaxer —good social position, ample wealth that lasted most if not all of his life, physical heftiness backed up by enormous muscular strength and pugilistic skill, a manner and voice usually obeyed without question, a genius for making innumerable friends—if not keeping them. He had a generous helping of histrionic ability and a psychological kink that enabled him to plan and execute his japes with deadly seriousness. He appeared to possess a certain mesmeric hold over his friends, at least when he wanted their assistance in some prank. Finally, he was well endowed with wit, cunning, and malice.

A grotesque, infallibly successful scamp? Yes, but a man of indisputable charm as well as of spleen, and he could switch them about in a trice! Above all, he had a ready-made target—what he felt to be the absurdity of his age, whether exhibited by individuals or the community at large. 'I am at war with pomposity,' he would declare.

It was whilst he was still up at Cambridge that Cole first achieved notoriety, by the famous 'Sultan of Zanzibar' escapade of 2 March 1905. Already he had played many minor jokes upon friend and foe alike, but now he wanted to hit the headlines. His accomplice was his friend and fellow undergraduate, Adrian Stephen, and each put up an idea for what they called 'something bigger'.

Stephen's suggestion, fired by the recent Zabern incident near the French frontier, was to secure for the two of them the uniforms of German army officers, take them to some township in Alsace-Lorraine on the Franco-German border, then take command of a detachment of German troops and march them across the border into France. The idea was deliberately to provoke 'an international incident', for it was hoped that the French would seize the miscreants and intern them, forcing the Kaiser to send one of his famous telegrams of protest. The idea of this is basically the same as that carried out a few years later by the ex-gaolbird of Koepenick.

However, Cole decided that such a hoax was both impracticable and likely to prove too costly. He felt that there were equally good targets awaiting deflation at home; and furthermore, of course, it wasn't a Cole idea. So the master hoaxer's own suggestion was adopted, and swiftly put into operation. The plan was to spoof the Town and Gown of Cambridge by a fake visit there of the Sultan of Zanzibar and his suite. Cole had obviously remembered a somewhat similar joke involving the 'Shah of Persia' some years before. He was directing his sardonic wit at the then excessive number of state visits to England by foreign royalties, minor and otherwise, with the attendant sycophantic reception by officialdom and the natives generally.

The real Sultan of Zanzibar was conveniently in England at the time, but at the last moment Cole seems to have funked the idea of actually impersonating the potentate himself. He pretended that as the Sultan was due for an audience with the King that day he was sending his brother and two cousins to do the honours at Cambridge. As Cole and Stephen, and two of their accomplices, Bowen Colthurst and Leland Buxton, were all up at the University and didn't want to be sent down, they naively decided to hoax only the Mayor and Corporation, not the University authorities. The fifth member of the troupe, the diminutive 'Dummer' Howard, was an Oxford man, chosen as being unlikely to be recognized at Cambridge and therefore ideal as the 'interpreter'.

A telegram was sent to Alderman Campkin, the Mayor, warning him of the imminent arrival of the dusky visitors and signed 'Lucas'—'because high colonial officials always bore that name'. Having arrayed themselves splendidly at a London theatrical costumiers, at Cole's expense, the five arrived by train and were met by Mr Whitehead, the un-suspecting Town Clerk, and taken by carriage to the Guild-hall, where a formal welcome from the Mayor and Corpora-tion awaited them. Oddly refusing the mayoral champagne (so as not to endanger their dark make-up), the five spent an entertaining hour or two bamboozling the Edwardian Establishment with confidence and glee, conversing by hand-signs (so as to avoid the language difficulty), and expressing their delight with continual salaams and 'violent gesticulations'.

They visited a charity bazaar that happened to be taking place that afternoon in the Guildhall. Cole, as the Sultan's brother (or uncle), made extensive 'purchases' from all the stalls without parting with any cash! They then emerged into the town, and visited some of the colleges. Sir Shane

Leslie, a contemporary of Cole's at Cambridge, remembers assisting at the opening of the big gates at King's 'for Cole's superb entry'. 'We managed to steer him from entering the Chapel,' adds Sir Shane. At Trinity the porters bared their heads and bowed low as the potentates arrived, but not as low as the guests salaamed before a carved bust of Queen Victoria. They toured the College, paying particular attention to a very untidy empty room which, so they were informed, was occupied by an absent student named Cole.

At last the time came for departure. Quite a crowd had now gathered at the Guildhall, and Cole distributed largesse among them before taking his leave of the Mayor. The party was escorted back to the station, but, having no wish to return to London, had to make a hurried escape through the platform crowds, out of the Great Northern entrance, into a couple of waiting hansoms and away out into the country and a friend's house. The four Cambridge men were back at Trinity next day, but not before their delighted hosts had received a gracious parting gesture: a touching memento, a personal gift from the Sultan himself. On the accompanying card it appeared he had written in his own hand: 'The dorsal fin from the Sacred Shark of Zanzibar —a token of everlasting remembrance.'

There is no doubt at all that Cambridge had been well and truly spoofed, although subsequently the offended dignitaries were not very ready to admit it. The truth emerged when the *Cambridge Daily News* wired the Carlton Hotel in London (where the real Sultan was staying) and learnt that His Eminence and suite had not left London on that day. Several know-alls then claimed that the party had seemed to know their way about the town and the colleges. The in-dignant Mayor declared he had not been entirely convinced that his visitors were genuine but had had to carry on as if they were until a hoax could be proved.

Cole kept calm—as always—and distributed copies of the photograph of the troupe he had had taken in London before the hoax began, signing them for the college porters and others: 'Mukasa Ali, Princeps Zanzibaris'. On the following Sunday, Alderman Campkin fulminated against the hoaxers in a sermon at the local Primitive Methodist Church, of which he was a lay preacher, and this was supported by a pompous leader in the *Cambridge Daily News* demanding instant punishment for the four Trinity men.

Adrian Stephen later revealed that Cole 'was determined to go to London and see what he could do to get publicity', and it was only a day or so before the whole thing was exposed in the *Daily Mail*. The London Press took it all as a good joke, but at Cambridge there were printed mutterings about 'a stupid hoax', 'unwarrantable conduct', 'supposed gentlemen', etc. The Mayor secretly demanded that the Vice-Chancellor send all four down. But wiser counsels prevailed and, as always, Cole got away with it, gleeful in the sure knowledge that all his barbs had found their targets.

The Sultan of Zanzibar hoax is worthy of detailed study by anyone seeking to absorb the lore of the now virtually extinct art of the practical joke. It was Cole's first masterpiece, and from it he learnt a number of important things. Costumes and disguises, if used, must be of first-rate quality, but the impersonation of exotics raises difficulties over language that must be overcome. Deflation of pomposity is very simple once a straightforward plan has been made, though extemporization must also be taken in stride. Publicity is essential for the complete success of any jape, and must include photographs which the newspapers can use. Confidence both grows and can be induced in accomplices. Above all, 'in audacity lies safety'. Horace de Vere Cole was to profit from these lessons for the rest of his life.

His art undoubtedly reached its peak with the classic 'Dreadnought' hoax of 7 February 1910. In its essentials it was a repetition of the Cambridge jest, but the target was much bigger—not merely the Royal Navy as such, but the whole absurd world of service protocol and pomposity. As with many of Cole's exploits, it was not without an ingredient of personal malice. The objective was none other than Admiral Sir W. W. Fisher (1875–1937), the Navy's 'Willie Fisher', who was Commander-in-Chief in the Mediterranean at the time of the Abyssinian crisis. He was a cousin of Adrian and Virginia Stephen (later the novelist Virginia Woolf) and, in Cole's fearless opinion, he urgently needed deflation.

Adrian Stephen declared that the whole idea of this famous escapade was in fact given to Cole by another naval officer, adding that 'those who afterwards made a to-do

For the same reason he bade them refuse all the traditional naval hospitality on board. Characteristically, however, once the formalities were over, he himself retired to the ward-room and enjoyed that hospitality, leaving the five to tour the ship and rely for communication upon an unholy mixture of gibberish, Virgil, and Homer concocted extempore by Stephen and nobly taken up by Buxton: 'Yembo inscara milu berango scutaea bonga astema hevashi shemal. Tahli bussor ahbat tahe aesque miss. Entaqui, mahai, kustufani. Erraema, fleet use . . .' and so on—a 'fine repertory of nonsense' that everyone on board took to be Abyssinian.

Miraculously, the afternoon wore on without a single slip being made, though there were several near squeaks and much odd behaviour, not least when Virginia Woolf's beard grew loose and she got the giggles—an incident explained away as the Abyssinian royal temperament. At each new sight the visitors raised eyes and arms heavenwards and chanted 'Bunga Bunga', a phrase soon to become a humorous national catchword, and destined to haunt Admiral May till the end of his career. By a pretty irony, also, *Dreadnought*'s bandmaster had no parts of the Abyssinian National Anthem, so the band played that of Zanzibar instead, with apologies!

On their return to London, exhausted though they were, Cole quickly unleashed a torrent of press publicity that soon whipped up the furore of indignation (or laughter) he had intended. Leader-writers and cartoonists had a field-day. One of Clarkson's assistants who had helped make up the hoaxers gave a newspaper interview in which he revealed that his clients had frequently uttered 'Bunga Bunga' to show their delight. In no time at all music-hall comedians were singing, to the tune of 'The Girl I Left Behind Me':

> When I went on board a Dreadnought ship
> Though I looked just like a costermonger,
> They said I was an Abyssinian prince
> Because I shouted 'Bunga Bunga'!

Parliamentary questions were asked, and prosecution of the offenders was widely urged, but no official retribution was ever meted out. The account of the visit was carefully expunged from *Dreadnought*'s logbook, and when Stephen and Grant heard a rumour that Admiral May was to be officially reprimanded they personally went to Whitehall to tender their apologies to Mr McKenna, the First Lord of the Admiralty, feeling that this might soften the blow about to be dealt to a distinguished officer already sixty-one. But McKenna would have none of it and bundled them curtly out of his room.

Unofficial retribution, on Fisher's directions, was put into action. Both Cole and Grant were subjected to ceremonial canings. A naval officer member of the Bath Club, to which Cole also belonged, was detailed to find the ringleader's exact weight from the attendants. Then an expert naval boxer of that weight called upon Cole in his rooms one night to take the Navy's revenge. Although a doughty scrapper himself, Cole confessed he took a terrific hiding that night, and the honour of the Senior Service was satisfied.

Perhaps only Admiral May never quite got over it. Whenever he went ashore someone was sure to cat-call 'Bunga Bunga' after him. He could never forget that at the end of that memorable day he had telegraphed the Admiralty: RECEPTION OF ABYSSINIAN PRINCES GREAT SUCCESS, to receive the immediate reply: WHAT ABYSSINIAN PRINCES?

This escapade cost Horace Cole, on his own admission, something like £4,000, and he never achieved anything quite so spectacularly perfect again. Early in 1919, however, he pulled off another very big and expensive hoax, about which little has been told. It was an attempt to exploit the immediate post-war political chaos, when the map of Europe was being redrawn and many minor monarchies had crumbled. Cole somehow managed to persuade a fatuous but extremely wealthy Englishman whose ignorance of world affairs was only matched by his appetite for prestige that the 'Crown of Croatia' was on the market. Furthermore, it was being anxiously sought by an American of even greater wealth. The victim took the bait at once.

Cole and some cronies took a fashionable house in Eaton Place, and transformed it at considerable expense into the 'Croat Legation'. Through intermediaries, and with great secrecy, the Englishman was induced to visit the Legation. After several fruitless interviews with underlings he was finally allowed to see the Croat Minister himself. Cole, acting the part as only he could, again used Willy Clarkson as disguiser, adding a darkened room with hints of eye trouble to avoid recognition. Although couched in diplomatic verbiage, the basic terms of the agreement reached were that the victim, being a great lover of all things Croatian and having lately contributed an astronomical sum to the Croat Treasury to rescue the country from bankruptcy, would on a day to be appointed receive the Crown and Regalia of that far-off kingdom from the grateful hands of a delegation of Croat bishops, statesmen, and generals, who were even now hurrying to London for that very purpose.

The dupe's vanity being well and truly tickled, he handed over his vast cheque, and on the appointed day arrived at the Legation in his limousine, clad, as seemed fitting for the occasion, in white tie and tails. Powdered footmen bowed and ushered their new 'ruler' through succeeding pairs of gilded double doors into the great drawing-room for the enthronement ceremony. But the 'delegation' waiting there to greet him, as the final doors were flung wide, was revealed to be Cole and a gang of cronies drinking champagne toasts to their victim's munificent cheque which was framed on the wall.

Incidentally, this jape was nearly revealed at the eleventh hour by a couple of real-life penniless Russian refugee officers whom Cole had hired to play the roles of Legation secretaries, speaking their native tongue. They went on strike for higher pay and threatened to let the cat out of the bag unless they got it. Fortunately, Cole's ample purse saved the day once more.

Horace Cole's great friend Augustus John gave a vivid pen-picture of him about this time in his autobiographical volume, *Chiaroscuro*:

> Horace Cole was at this time in his prime. The great practical joker, in full possession of good looks and an ample fortune, presented to the world the interesting spectacle of a pseudo Anglo-Irish aristocrat impersonating the God of Mischief. A plentiful crop of white, but by no means venerable, hair crowned his almost classic headpiece which was, in addition, furnished with upstanding moustaches in the style of the late Kaiser Wilhelm. His fine blue eyes blazed with malice and self-assurance.

During his heyday Cole lived a semi-Bohemian existence, rich in friends and in opportunities for playing jokes upon them. He was a regular diner at the old Café Royal when it was the haunt of artists, wits, and London's lost Bohemia, and he was ever ready to play some mad prank, often at a moment's notice. When some irritated fellow diner quoted at him Shakespeare's lines about 'How ill white hairs become a fool and jester' Cole bowed submissively, walked out of the restaurant, and returned an hour later with his huge mane and whiskers dyed a bright vermilion. 'Better?' he asked.

On another occasion as he was leaving the Café Royal after lunch he encountered a group of navvies at work on the road outside. They genuinely mistook him, as others had done, for Ramsay MacDonald, who was then the first Labour Prime Minister. (Aided by a physical resemblance and great skill at mimicking MacDonald's harsh Scottish accent, Cole had exploited the situation before, even to the extent of having cards printed in the politician's name.) The supposed Prime Minister was asked by the navvies for a speech. This was altogether too good a chance for Cole to miss. He let forth a lively tirade on the pavement—but of the wrong political hue. He began with the customary platitudes, but gradually worked up to a hectic climax, damning the trade unions and declaring that as from that moment he was no longer associated with the rascally and depraved Labour Party. His audience, at first suspicious, finally became menacing, and Cole was forced to escape into a passing taxi. Even then his fiendish wit did not desert him, for he yelled at the driver: 'Number Ten Downing Street—and hurry!'

A grotesque giant amid many pigmies, Horace de Vere Cole was indeed (as his *Times* obituarist put it) 'at one time one of the best-known men in London'. It was he, as everyone knew, who had dug a trench right across Piccadilly outside the Cavalry Club, aided by some friends disguised as navvies. Not everyone knew that he had taken all the front rooms in the Ritz in order to watch the ensuing chaos, which lasted for three days.

One of his ideas of an afternoon's fun was to lie in bed fully dressed in a furniture-shop window with his boots sticking out at the end. It was Cole, too, who accosted two City gentlemen, handed each of them one end of a surveyor's tape ('. . . have to re-align the kerb . . . might I prevail upon your time for a few moments . . .'), and, with each man invisible to the other round a corner, darted away to watch the fun from a safe distance.

It could truthfully be said of Cole that his enemies never slept peacefully at night, so awful were some of his methods of revenge. He would think nothing of ordering from thirty shops thirty grand pianos to be delivered to an enemy's address at 11 a.m. on one and the same day, or arranging the most elaborate funeral hearse, complete with drapes and flowers, to call for some still much alive acquaintance who had offended him. When invention flagged, Cole would knock off the hat of some choleric passer-by so that it fell into a muddy gutter, and the blame attached itself miraculously to Cole's innocent and astonished companion.

'Molar' Cole, as his closest friends knew him, was congenitally deaf from childhood to some degree, but invariably pretended to be more so than he really was. This led to untold japes, and frequently enabled him to escape the fury of his victims. It also, or so he fancied, enabled him to ignore the niceties of convention and use his naturally booming voice in public with sardonic effect. 'Who's that female with old So-and-so?' he would bellow in a restaurant. 'She looks like a sack of potatoes.'

In 1918 he married a seventeen-year-old heiress from Co. Galway named Denise Daly, and they honeymooned, not entirely inappropriately, at Blarney Castle. Her own account of their courtship and early married life has been described as 'unbelievably comic'—and largely unprintable. Indeed, although some of Cole's hoaxes have been completely forgotten and unrecorded, others are unlikely to achieve the dignity of print because of their Rabelaisian cast. In 1911 Horace Cole's sister Anne married a Birmingham city councillor named Neville Chamberlain, but mercifully the master joker does not seem to have made the future Prime Minister the victim of any of his pranks. Although she brought up his daughter Valerie, after the failure of his first marriage, Mrs Chamberlain saw very little of her preposterous brother.

Not all of Cole's seemingly unlimited wealth went on his jests. He became a knowledgeable connoisseur of art and built up a valuable collection of modern pictures. He also wrote verse that has been described as delightful. He was a great walker, roaming over half of Europe, ceaselessly playing his tricks even in the remotest places, where they were usually not appreciated. The French especially responded to his particular brand of humour with violent disgust. Indeed, one of the very few occasions when he did not get away with one of his practical jokes was during a visit to Corsica, where a fisherman victim pulled a gun and shot Cole in the leg.

Towards the end of his life, which was spent largely in France, word got round that Cole had reformed, and was devoting himself to the more serious things of life. In fact, he retained his wit until the end. Almost the last thing he did in England was to visit the Tower of London to see if there were any hoax, no matter how complicated, by which he could temporarily purloin the Crown Jewels. For once he had to admit defeat.

The end came suddenly from heart failure on 25 February 1936, at Honfleur, where he was staying with his second wife Mavis (later to marry Sir Mortimer Wheeler) and his young son Tristan (now, by a supreme irony, a rising officer in the Royal Navy). The master joker was buried in England. Among the mourners was Augustus John, faithful to the last:

> I went in hopes of a miracle—or a joke. As the coffin was slowly lowered into the grave, in dreadful tension I awaited the moment for the lid to be lifted, thrust aside, and a well-known figure to leap out with an ear-splitting yell. But my old friend disappointed me this time.

Mr Schenk
and his Draperies

BY CUTHBERT EDGE

SOME YEARS ago I came across two large volumes issued by
a certain Mr Charles Schenk of New York, one in the year
1899, the other in 1902. To my surprise I find today that
they are rather rare, and I ask myself why. The first volume
is a German edition—or rather a single German title page
clapped on to the untitled New York-printed plates:
Malerische Akstudien, it reads, *photographische Aufnahmen
nach der Natur und zwar einzelner Körpertheile und ganzer
Figuren*, which may be rendered roughly as 'Artistic nude
studies: photographs from nature, including parts of the
body and the whole figure.' Each plate bears the words
'Copyright, 1899, by Chas. Schenk, publisher, N.Y.' The
other volume is boldly and simply entitled in English
Draperies in Action, published by Charles Schenk.

Try as I may, I cannot lay either of them by their biblio-
graphical heels; nor can I discover if there was ever any text
to give the reader (or rather gazer) a clue or *rationale* concerning the splendid visions that follow. The whole caboodle
—taking the two volumes together—must have been meant
as a serious contribution to the home study of art. The
majority of the more than four hundred photographs—
reproduced in fine photogravure—are of women, but a
few males (both *Körpertheile* and *ganzer Figuren*) are littered
hairily about in between.

I said above that they provide 'splendid visions': so they
do. Monumental posing and composition of the nude, and
even the drapery—frozen by some trick we know not how—
is admirably related to the bodies they envelop or reveal.
And what bodies! Splendid is certainly the word for them,
sex-appeal and all. They knew how to build women in those
days.

205

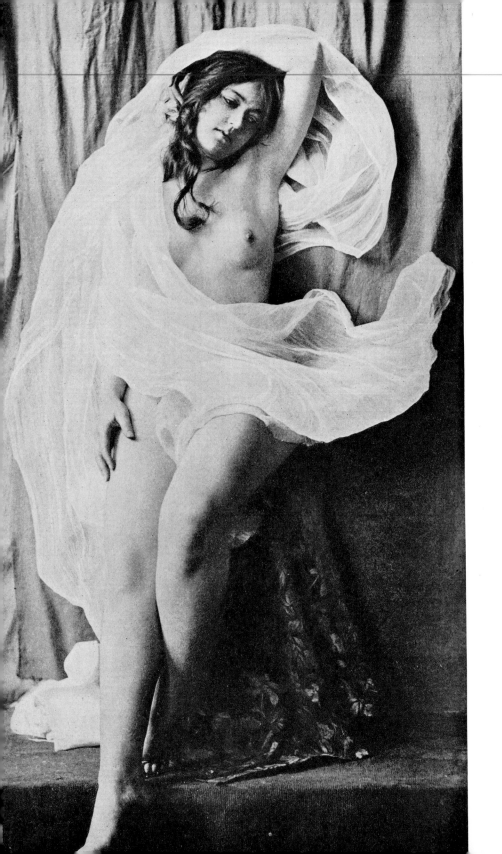

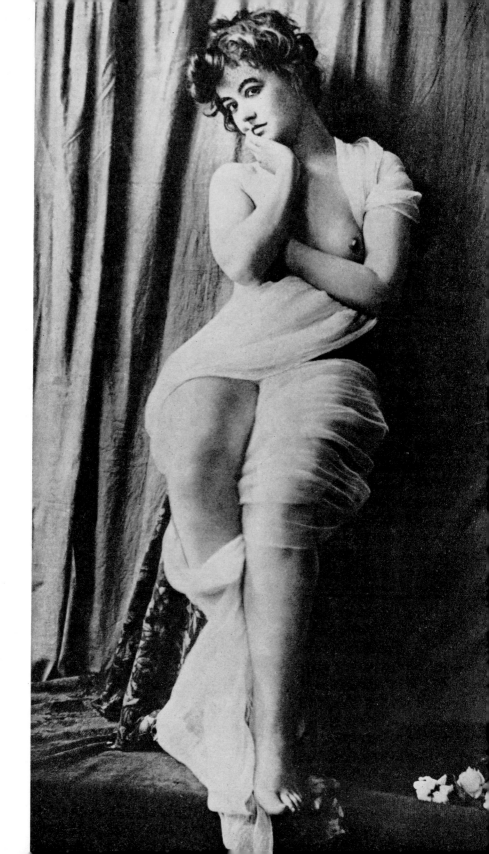

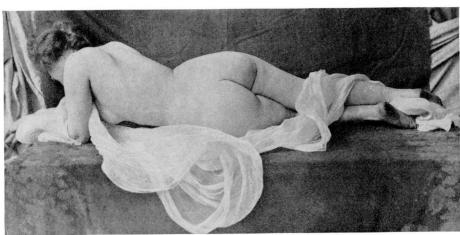

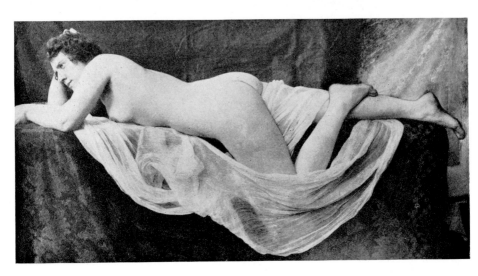

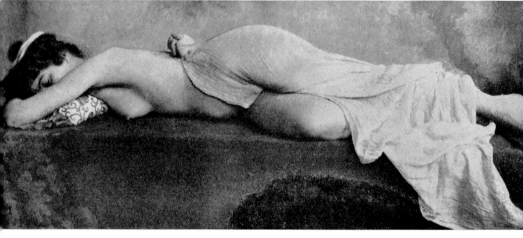

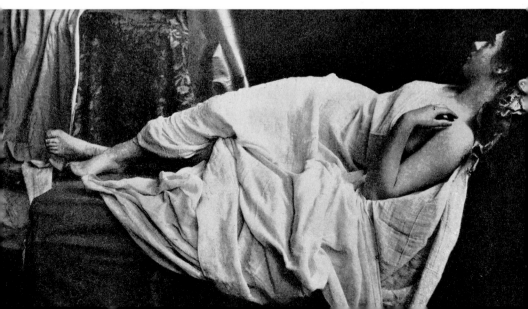

1

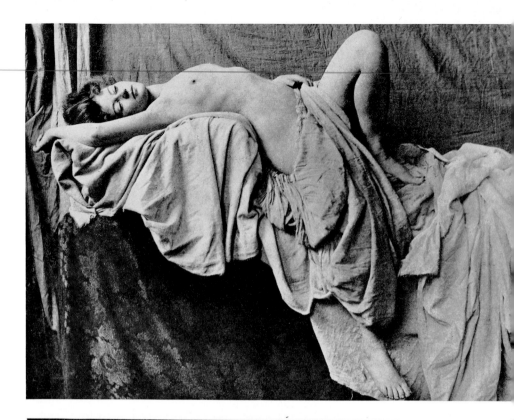

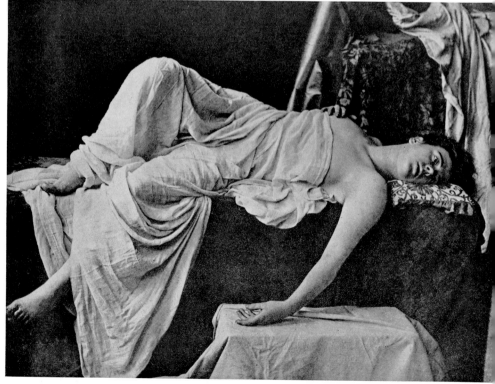

5

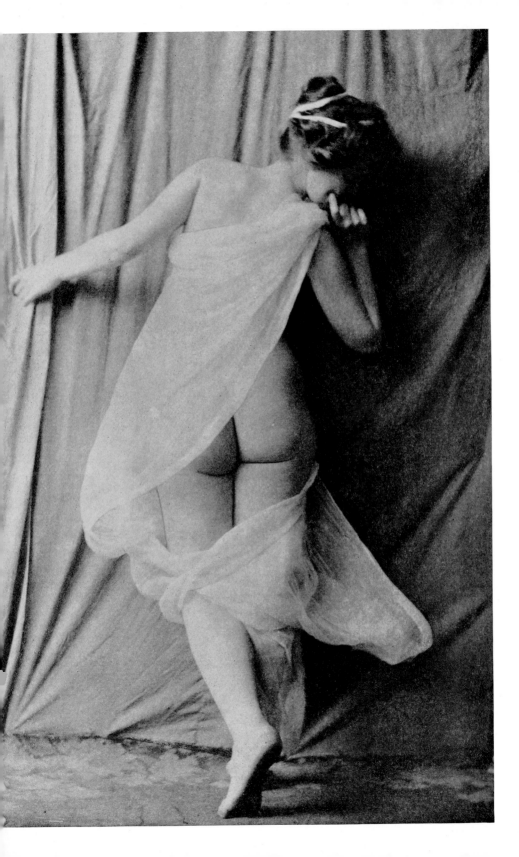

The Social History of the

the

DUEL

BY

AMORET & CHRISTOPHER SCOTT

IN FRANCE during the seventeenth century 8,000 men of noble blood fell in duels in a period of twenty years. So universally was this method of settling disputes accepted in England that not one survivor of a duel was executed for murder in a period of 200 years from about 1700. Eighteenth-century Ireland was 'dotted all over with fields of honour'. In the Roaring 'Forties few cowboys of the Far West lived to see thirty, since they were either shot, or hanged for shooting someone else.

During the seventeenth and eighteenth centuries the code of behaviour governing the preliminaries and the actual meeting for the duel was observed with the utmost precision. The French 'Code de Duel' was drawn up and signed by a representative body of French noblemen with as much care as if the subject had been the Constitution itself. The equivalent in the English-speaking world was the Irish 'Code Duello', adopted with all pomp and ceremony at the Clonmel Summer Assizes in 1777. This was popularly known as the Twenty-six Commandments. Rule Number 9 directed 'all

imputations of cheating at play, races etc. to be considered equivalent to a blow, but may be reconciled after one shot, on admitting the falsehood and begging pardon publicly'. Rule Number 10 enjoined 'any insult to a lady under a gentleman's care or protection to be considered as by one degree a greater offence than if given to the gentleman personally, and to be regarded accordingly'.

The essentials of both French and English (or rather Irish) codes were virtually identical, and were considered binding upon 'all right-thinking and honourable gentlemen'. It is important to realize that duelling, as a means of settling affairs of any kind, was strictly a matter for social equals. Voltaire, a bourgeois (his father was a notary), in 1726 presumed so far upon his international reputation as to send a challenge to the Chevalier de Rohan. The Chevalier, acting entirely in accordance with the accepted code of behaviour, replied by sending six of his servants to give Voltaire a thrashing. The writer persisted, and found himself in the Bastille, where he stayed for six months before he was virtually deported from France. One did not meddle lightly with the Code de Duel in those days.

Between equals a hasty word, a misconceived gesture, a

difference of opinion on the colour of a riband, a collision in a waltz—all these were enough cause for a man to 'name his friend' (an obligatory part of the challenge). From that moment on, the machine of the Code bore the parties inexorably towards each other, as they trod delicately between such pitfalls as the crime of allowing any relation of the first degree to serve as their second, or the decision as to whether the offence was a simple one, or one of an insulting nature, or one with personal acts of violence, each of which demanded a different outcome.

What kind of people stand out as individual members of the multitude who crossed rapiers in the Bois de Boulogne at dawn; who squinted along their shaking pistol-barrels, fifteen paces apart, at Chalk Farm; who walked steadily towards each other down the long, dusty street of Dodge City, hands hovering over the butts of their six-shooters? The majority were composed very largely of French army officers, for several uncomplicated reasons. Fighting was their trade, however much they might corset and pomade themselves, and a sword was as familiar to them as a hammer to a blacksmith. And of course it must be remembered that from the days of Caesar's legions to the onset of the French Revolution everybody who was anybody *was* an army officer anyway. The preponderance of soldiers amongst duellists is not surprising.

But the others, the nuggets glinting in the mud of uniformity, who were they? Irishmen—a lot of Irishmen. Authors, sensitive to criticism. Journalists, sensitive to nothing, but always eager to put the name of their journals in the public eye even if they themselves died in the attempt (a rare occurrence). A few clergymen, involved in the most unlikely affairs, often over women (although Ignatius Loyola, the founder of the Jesuits, carried militant Christianity to the extent of calling out a man who denied the divinity of our Lord, and running him through). Several women, battling openly one with another or disguised as men. Politicians. German students. And a curious selection of individual oddities, such as the two Russians who at the ages of 100 and 103 fought a duel over a woman in St Petersburg; they both collapsed after an exchange of shots, but when their seconds rushed to their bodies they were found to be merely in the last stages of senile exhaustion.

Throughout the years Irishmen have figured largely in duels of all kinds. During the days of the old Parliament in College Green, Dublin, the Provost of Trinity College once directed a young student who had asked his advice about a course of legal study to buy a case of pistols before anything else, 'as', he added, 'they will get you along faster than Fearne or Blackstone'. Daniel O'Connell was involved in one duel in his life, but it must be said there are the strongest suspicions that it was engineered against him by his political enemies. A certain Count d'Esterre was a member of the

Dublin Corporation in 1815 when O'Connell referred to it in terms which, for an Irishman, were disparaging but mild. The Count immediately challenged O'Connell, who was unable to avoid the issue without destroying his reputation. The meeting at Bishop's Court in Kildare ended with the Count, a well-known shot, lying dead on the grass, and his opponent, who had scarcely held a pistol in his hand before, unharmed. The remorse which d'Esterre's death occasioned in O'Connell never left him for the rest of his life, in spite of the strong rumour that the Count had actually been imported to Eire with the sole intention of finding an excuse for challenging O'Connell.

In about 1780 the brilliant Irish wit John Philpot Curran fought four duels in succession. In one of them his opponent was a truly enormous man, a certain Mr Egan. When they took up their pistols, the latter complained that it was like putting up a turf-stack before a razor, to which Curran replied: 'I'll tell you what it is, Mr Egan: as I wish to take no advantage of you, let my size be chalked out upon your side, and I am quite content that every shot which hits outside that mark shall go for nothing.' Both men in this case fired to miss and they left the field as friends.

The vast Charles James Fox, too, when advised by his second to stand sideways in the recommended manner in order to present the smallest possible target to his opponent (a Mr Adam), remarked cheerfully: 'Why, I'm as thick one way as the other,' and fired his pistol deliberately wide of Adam. Adam fired and hit Fox—he could scarcely miss him—but without doing much damage.

The one rule observed throughout the centuries and the world (except perhaps in the Wild West) was that the choice of weapons belonged to the challenged party. This left a loophole through which many an ingenious gentleman managed to wriggle, still clutching his honour to him with both hands as he left. One example from Germany and one from the United States will illustrate this. The German case involved no less a person than the Iron Chancellor himself, Bismarck, who challenged a Russian professor, Virchow, after some real or imagined slight. Virchow, who scarcely knew one end of a gun from the other, accepted the challenge, adding that since it was his privilege to choose the weapons, he had decided upon sausages. Two sausages, one of which was infected with the germs of an unpleasant disease, were to be placed on plates in front of them. Bismarck would choose and eat one, and Virchow would then eat the other. Bismarck called off the challenge.

At much about the same time a certain Parson Brownlow published an article in the *Knoxville* (Tennessee) *Whig* to which a reader took such exception that he sent a challenge on the spot. Brownlow replied as follows: 'Yes, sir, I accept the challenge; and since I am the challenged party, it is my right to choose the weapons, time and place. As the place, I select the nastiest hog-pen in the vicinity of Knoxville; time, just after the first July shower; weapons, dung forks.

The man who stays in the pit longest to win the fight.' The challenger's stomach failed him.

It is an historical fact that one challenged gentleman did indeed choose as his weapons custard pies at six paces. He was an American reporter; the duel did not take place.

These particular encounters fizzled out without so much as a spark. If matters got to the stage of the principals actually meeting, well-intentioned seconds sometimes did their best to avert bloodshed by tampering with the weapons. Sir Thomas Moore, the poet, and his opponent Francis Jeffrey, editor of the *Edinburgh Review*, were arrested just before they set about each other one morning in 1806; their pistols were found to contain not bullets, but paper pellets, which was considered highly appropriate.

But if the spirit was smarting sufficiently to allow the challenger to agree to 'weapons' which the rest of the world thought ridiculous, then blood could flow as easily as it did in more orthodox cases. In 1843 two young Frenchmen named Lenfant and Melfant quarrelled in the course of a game of billiards, and agreed to settle their differences there and then, using the nearest convenient articles—billiard balls. They drew lots to decide who should have the red ball and first throw. Melfant won the red ball and they retired to the garden, where they took up their positions facing each other twelve paces apart. Melfant drew back his arm, said: 'I am going to kill you at the first throw,' and threw the ball with all his force. It struck Lenfant in the middle of the forehead; he dropped dead. The survivor was arrested, tried for murder and convicted of manslaughter.

Probably the ultimate in tragi-comedy was the case of M. de Grandpré and M. de Pique, who in 1808 both fell madly in love with a *prima donna* at the Imperial Opera. The rivalry blossomed until a challenge was issued and accepted, the agreed conditions being that each party should supply himself with a blunderbuss and a balloon and that the hand of the lady should be fought for above the roofs of Paris. The day came, the gallant gentlemen and their respective seconds climbed each into the basket of their balloons, tethered at a distance of about half a mile: ballast was flung out and they rose into the morning sky. For some time they remained at much the same distance, the light wind blowing them both along at a similar speed. But then, when they were some hundreds of feet above the ground, a gust carried them within range of each other. M. de Grandpré's discharge tore a huge hole in the envelope of his rival's balloon, which immediately fell like a stone to the ground, carrying M. le Pique (and his unfortunate second as well) to his death. One might at least have expected that the victor in this aerial battle would have got his reward. But the astringent truth is that the lady thoroughly disapproved of the whole affair, and subsequently married someone else.

M. de Grandpré had the sense to fire at his opponent's gas-bag rather than his person, and his aim was true. The same cannot be said of some other participants in affairs of honour. In an American duel in 1853 between Senator William Gwin and Representative J. W. McCorckle, the only result of the first exchange of shots was that a donkey grazing half a mile away fell dead. In about 1780, two Frenchmen stood back-to-back in the approved manner, marched apart to fifteen paces, turned, and fired, only to see each one's second drop dead to the ground. '*Mon Dieu!*' said a spectator, 'what a lucky escape!'

A good many lucky escapes are in fact recorded in eye-witness accounts of duels throughout the centuries. Sir Jonah Barrington and Leonard McNally once exchanged shots in Phoenix Park, Dublin. McNally cried: 'I am hit'; the attendant surgeon pulled up his shirt and found that the ball had struck the buckles of his gallows (braces) and ricocheted off without touching the skin. 'By Gad, Mac,' said Barrington's second, 'you are the only rogue I ever knew that was saved by the gallows.' A good many five-franc pieces saved their owners from injury or death; an apt comment after one such occasion was made by M. Mery, second to Armestée Archard in his meeting with Charles Blanc: 'That's what I call money well invested.'

Between the beginning of the sixteenth century and the middle of the nineteenth scores of books were written upon every aspect of the code and science of duelling—who to challenge, how to challenge, where to fight and what to fight with: in short, how to conduct oneself at every moment and occasion between the first hot flush of anger and the moment of truth when your opponent lay dying upon the ground. In one much-admired English work you were advised to invite friends to dinner on the night before the

meeting, to laugh away the evening over a bottle of port but not to drink too much. You should take an amusing book to bed, 'one of Sir Walter Scott's novels for example'. In the morning have your servant call you at five with strong coffee. If you were married, it was inadvisable to disturb your wife or children. If you felt nervous on the way to the meeting place, stop and take 'a bottle of soda water flavoured with a small wine-glass of brandy'. And this: 'I cannot impress upon an individual too strongly the propriety of remaining perfectly calm and collected when hit: and if he dies, to go off with as good a grace as possible.' Alternatively, if the reader is lucky enough to see his 'ball take effect, a salute and an expression of regret should always precede his quitting the field'.

We have some excellent literary records of the feelings of duellists before the day. Disraeli, in *Vivian Grey*, writes:

> You pass the morning at your second's apartment, pacing his drawing room with a quivering lip and uncertain step.

At length he enters with an answer, and while he reads you endeavour to look easy, with a countenance merry with the most melancholy smile. You have no appetite for dinner, but you are too brave not to appear at table; and you are called out after the second glass by the arrival of your solicitor, who comes to make your will. You pass a restless night and rise in the morning as bilious as a Bengal general.

Byron, no stranger to duels himself, caught a later moment:

> It has a strange, quick jar upon the ear
> That cocking of a pistol when you know,
> A moment more will bring the sights to bear
> Upon your person . . . twelve yards off or so.

Although the English and the Irish went to immense trouble to conduct their duels with all due propriety, the French, there is no doubt, had a rather special facility in dealing with their honour which foreigners were unable to match. This was true even when the affairs came to nothing.

Voiture, the French poet, was challenged over some petty matter and replied as follows: 'The game is not equal: you are big and I am little; you can fight and I cannot; you are brave and I am not. However, if you want to kill me, I will consider myself dead.' And consider this incident, which took place at the end of the eighteenth century in the gardens of the Palace of Versailles. St Foix, a famous duellist of the day, sauntered up to an officer of the guard and said: 'You smell like a goat.'

'Sir!' cried the scandalized man, drawing his sword.

'Put up your sword, you foolish fellow, put up your sword; for if you kill me you will not smell any better, and if I kill you you will smell a great sight worse.'

There were, of course, occasions on which a challenge was given and accepted with the most deadly seriousness, and in the knowledge that neither party would be satisfied until one of them was killed. In such cases there was an unofficial code of rules which ensured that this result was achieved. In France it was the custom to lock the two, each with a dagger, in a coach with the blinds drawn; it was then slowly driven three times round a square near the Bois de Boulogne before the doors were unlocked. Another type of duel *à l'outrance* called upon the men to choose at random from two pistols, only one of which was loaded, held by a third party behind his back. The antagonists then each took hold of the corner of a handkerchief with his left hand and, standing toe to toe, fired on a signal.

In America certainly the most famous duel to the death was that between General Andrew Jackson and Charles Dickinson, fought on 30 May 1806, near Adairville, Tennessee. The names of both men were known to the whole country, both were crack shots, and each was determined to kill the other. (The occasion was a deliberate insult by Dickinson to Jackson's wife.) Both were calm and confident; Dickinson amused his associates on the way to the meeting by showing his extraordinary skill with a pistol. The two men faced each other with pistols pointing to the ground. Upon the signal, they raised them; Dickinson fired. A puff of dust flew from the breast of Jackson's coat, and he raised his left arm and placed it tightly across his chest, still standing firm. 'Great God, have I missed him?' cried Dickinson. Jackson then raised his pistol again with great deliberation, pulled the trigger—and the weapon stopped at half-cock. Lowering it, the General pulled back the hammer, took aim again, and fired. Dickinson reeled to the ground, dying. Only then was it seen that one of Jackson's shoes was filled with blood: the first bullet had hit him in the chest, breaking two ribs. He afterwards told his second that even had he been shot through the heart he would have stayed alive long enough to kill his opponent.

In England, at least, duelling pistols enjoyed nothing like the length of fashionable popularity attributed to them by romantic fiction. Their vogue was between about 1770 and 1840. Money that was spent upon fine pistols was expended not for their looks—they tended to be plain, with the minimum of engraving and chasing which could glint in the light and provide a mark for your opponent to aim at—but for their reliability and accuracy; no man taking his life in his right hand in this way wanted to experience the dreaded flash in the pan. Makers such as Joseph Manton, Durs Egg or Wogdon received fifty guineas for a pair of duellers.

In 1840 Queen Victoria signified her displeasure with 'the barbarous practice', and it took the Commons no more than a month to amend the Articles of War to make duelling a court-martial offence for officers.

The last duel of any kind recorded in England was no later than 1 July 1843.

In the United States duels of a kind were still being fought well into the present century, usually under cowboy rules and with heavy revolvers as weapons. In that country they had the benefit of the conflict between federal and state law, and such encounters almost invariably took place within a few yards of the state border, to allow the survivor to escape the consequences.

In Europe, however, matters were, and are, different. In 1947 an Italian deputy issued a challenge to a political opponent; the subsequent duel with swords lasted for nearly an hour, and ended only when both were too exhausted to continue. In 1948 two French ministers fought a pistol duel in Paris. There is no indication that the hazards of a hasty word or an ill-conceived gesture are any the less today; if you are a man of quick temper and you propose to cross the Channel this year, you would be well advised to take with you your favourite weapon—and, of course, a friend.

The Gold Rush

BY TUDOR EDWARDS

IT IS a pity that no Gustave Doré accompanied the bands of Argonauts that hit the Yukon trail of 1898 in the greatest of all gold booms. Such an observer would have left a unique pictorial record that might have done much to confirm—or explode—the near-mythical stories of the death and dread of the Klondike and the fabulous life of Dawson City. True, there was a handful of literary men there, among them Jack London and Robert W. Service. Jack London made little gold, and that only later from his *Call of the Wild*. Service was too busy to hunt nuggets, clerking in Dawson's Bank of Commerce and writing poetry in log cabins. 'It isn't the gold that I'm wanting so much as just finding the gold', he wrote. Perhaps had he prospected more his verses would have held less poetic licence, for some survivors say that 'them writing fellows' exaggerated, that there never was a Dangerous Dan McGrew. . . .

The legend began in the summer of 1896 when roughneck George Washington Carmack and Indian Skookum Jim, out for a day's salmon-fishing in the creek now called Bonanza, idly filled their pans with gravel—and struck gold. The staking and recording of their claims sent many men in the Canadian north scurrying to the various Klondike creeks, but soon winter ice sealed the earth until another spring. Communications were slow, and it was not until early in 1898 that the real significance of the gold-strike was revealed.

In that year two small ships sailed down the Yukon River to the sea. Aboard them were close on seventy wealthy men who less than a year earlier had been desperate paupers and who now carried with them the combined wealth of a million dollars in gold-dust. One ship reached Seattle, where newspapers picked up the story, and by the time that the other vessel had reached San Francisco the secret was out. The news flashed round the world and set the Yukon aflame. The great trek northward began.

Some went overland from the east, travelling down the Mackenzie Valley and across the mountains. Most arrived from the south, and thousands sailed from Seattle up the Pacific coast to land at the mushroom town of Skagway, then in United States territory and unprotected by the North-West Mounted Police as the Yukon was. Skagway was as lawless a place as ever existed in Hollywood celluloid. Most men in the far north honoured the stakes and property of others, with a strict regard for meum and tuum, but not so Soapy Smith. He was the mobster-dictator of Skagway, cheating, robbing, and murdering until he was finally shot down. The gangsterdom of Skagway was only the first hazard to be encountered by the thickening legion of gold-seekers. Having got safely out of Skagway with necessary supplies for about two months, they had to climb over a mountain range, descend to a lake on the other side, build boats, and sail six hundred miles down rivers and lakes to Dawson City.

Over the Chilkoot Pass early that year crawled a long almost endless human caterpillar. It was a slow, strenuous climb in single file over ice and snow, carrying packs with tents, bedding, provisions, and personal possessions, and leading heavily laden horses and even some goats and cows.

Thousands of horses stumbled and fell into the gorge or were swept away by avalanches. This stretch came to be known as Dead Horse Canyon. Many human beings met the same fate, but the lure of gold drew the others on.

Mrs George Black, who crossed the Chilkoot that year, later recalled the journey:

> As the day advanced the trail became steeper, the air warmer, and footholds without support impossible. I shed my sealskin jacket. I cursed my hot, high buckram collar, my tight heavily boned corsets, my long corduroy skirt, my full bloomers which I had to hitch up with every step. We clung to stunted pines, spruce roots, jutting rocks. In some places the path was so narrow that, to move at all, we had to use our feet tandem fashion. Above, only the granite walls. Below, death leering at us.

There seems little doubt that hundreds died on what has been called 'the worst trail this side of Hell', but it was not from starvation or gun-play, as Service suggested, but from foul water, from disease and spinal meningitis. Yet was it really as bad as all that? After all, Mike Mahoney carried a piano over the Chilkoot for a theatrical company playing in Dawson, and Bull Ballantyne carried another.

The summit of the Chilkoot reached, the descent to Lake Bennett began, where, in a magnificent mountain arena, the adventurers struck camp. Here they built and provisioned boats for the long voyage to the Klondike, mainly scows or flat-bottomed craft, but also canoes, sail-boats, and even rafts. Weeks later, when the ice had melted, the strange rag-and-bobtail armada swept down the Yukon River. Behind them came others, month after month, until the north was frozen up again. The scow that carried Mrs George Black and her companions was registered at the R.C.M.P. post as No. 14,405. Now the frail vessels passed through Miles Canyon, a narrow race between high stone cliffs where the White Horse Rapids swept over hidden rocks that barely broke the surface. It is not surprising that many were drowned there, for these were no experienced watermen. Yet people in the north scoff and say that lumbermen could ride *logs* through rougher water than the White Horse Rapids. And, anyway, what was to prevent them from landing just above the rapids, portaging their boats along the bank, and re-embarking farther down?

Another fortnight and the Argonauts would reach the shanty-town known as Dawson City at the confluence of the Yukon and Klondike Rivers, a ramshackle backwoods metropolis 2,000 miles from civilization. In 1898 it was going up fast, the tents and tin shacks being replaced by squat buildings of stout logs with stuccoed dummy fronts. Before the end of the century there was a floating population of some thirty thousand, with five churches, a hospital and convent, two banks, many hotels, and innumerable shops and places of entertainment. The main street, never much more than a dirt road with duckboards for pavements, fronted the Yukon River, its shores piled with black, ice-polished boulders, and was called, simply, Front Street. Along it, as thick as beads in a chaplet, were the hotels, dance-halls, bars, and gaming saloons. For a while Dawson was the Las Vegas of the north, the magnet that drew not only the gold prospectors, the trappers, and fur-traders, and the Indians in caribou parkas and pearl-stitched moccasins, but also the professional gamblers and the bawdy ladies.

From Dawson the gold-seekers, sartorially bizarre in fur hats and parkas and the strangest mixture of clothing, went out with dog-driven sledges to prospect in the various creeks: the Bonanza, Eldorado, Hunker, Gold Run, Sulphur, Quartz, and the rest. In summer they were a prey to mosquitoes, and winter, when it was often seventy degrees below zero, brought frostbite. Certainly it was a hard, empty country—'the cussedest land that I know . . . the white land locked tight as a drum', as Service put it. There they clawed at the frozen earth and thawed it with great fires, inch by inch, heating boulders to white heat, rolling them into the hole and out again until a shaft took shape.

It was possible for a digger to pan £5,000 worth of gold or more in a month. Sometimes he gave up and sold his claim for a song, and it yielded a fortune to the buyer. Ed Anderson made a lucky strike, but in the wild celebrations that followed in the fabulous Flora Dora saloon he was hit on the head with a champagne bottle and lost his memory. He spent the rest of his life looking for that strike, without success. Some grew rich and sailed away. Others, as fast as they made gold, spent it in Dawson, the oasis of this northern desert. They spilled their gold-dust on the bars, drank, brawled, and whored, and then returned to the creeks, broke, to begin shovelling all over again.

There were others who grew rich without a pick and shovel, for Dawson was filled with confidence-men and card-sharpers, with camp-followers, harlots, and dancing-girls. The clapboard façades of the places of entertainment were fancifully decorated with fluted pillars, classical pediments, and rococo scrolls. The saloon of the Savoy dance-hall had a fifty-foot hand-carved mahogany bar, paintings of nudes, and lustrous chandeliers. On the stage at the end of the dance-floor the 'girls' danced the Can-Can, the shapely legs, despite, it would seem, not a few elephantine buttocks, kicking and pirouetting above the sourdoughs' heads to the music of Offenbach, with flashes of pink thighs above satin-gartered stockings and ruffled lingerie.

It was an heroic and lecherous age. It was the age of the music-hall, of Grant Allen's *The Woman Who Did*, of Kipling's jingoism. Even in Dawson the spirit of the 'nineties and *fin de siècle* prevailed. Dawson, in fact, might have come straight out of *The Yellow Book*.

It was at the Savoy that Klondike Kate queened it. This red-headed convent-educated beauty came up from the booths of Manhattan's Coney Island to rule the dance-floors and saloons of Dawson. Often she wore a Worth gown sparkling with diamonds. Worth dressed the Empress Eugénie and the Princess Metternich, and what was good enough for them was good enough for Klondike Kate (though the gown probably came from Madame Tremblay's shop opposite Dawson's Palace Theatre).

There were other dance-halls, among them the Monte Carlo, Tivoli, Orpheum, Nugget, Palace, and Flora Dora with its troupe of Floradora Girls in their picture hats, tight bodices with mutton-chop sleeves, and long skirts sweeping to the footlights, for all these places had a stage at the end of the hall. The Palace, built in 1898 by Arizona Charlie, was the only legitimate theatre, and here touring companies played *East Lynne* and *The Lady of the Camellias* to the ladies of the town, glittering in their Paris gowns from Madame Tremblay's and shedding their tears on the shoulders of their husky menfolk, who had donned collars and ties for the evening.

Each dance-hall employed close on a hundred girls to

keep the gold flowing from the prospectors' pockets. These girls made at least $100 a night (a dollar a dance and a rake-off on the drinks). In addition, the whoopee-making sour-doughs loaded them with gifts, with gold nuggets which the girls wore in their hair, on necklaces and belts. They were literally weighed down with raw gold worth $16 an ounce—Klondike Kate not infrequently made $500 in a night, and her corsage was a beach of gold nuggets.

'Of the wiles and the gold-tooth smiles of a dance-hall wench beware,' sang Robert Service. They were not all gold-toothed, however. Diamond-Tooth Gertie had a sparkling diamond set in her front teeth. These dancing-girls have passed into history. There was Oregon Mare, who whinnied like a horse, and Lime-Juice Lil, who had a passion for that cordial, and there was Spanish Jeanette and Sweet Marie. Fortunes were lost for the smiles of some of these belles. Their morals were no better than they should be, and the rewards were rich, tempting, and easily come by. Mabel LaRose, a French-Canadian show-girl, sold herself for one winter as housekeeper and mistress. She climbed on to the bar of the Monte Carlo and auctioned herself off—she went at $5,000.

Indeed, it would seem that it was the women who got the gold in the end. A Floradora Girl named Lou bought a small piece of land on the edge of the town for less than £100, and shortly afterwards, when gold had been struck there, sold it for a hundred times that sum. The vogue among the Dawson 'girls' was to consider proposals of marriage if their weight in gold was forthcoming as a gift. Swiftwater Bill Gates, a dishwasher who struck it rich on Claim No. 13 and then opened a bar in the town, offered Gussie Lamaire her weight in gold to marry him. The scales tipped $3,000 worth but she still held out. Since Gussie had a passion for eggs (which cost $16 a dozen), Swiftwater collected every egg in Dawson at a loss of $2,000 and laid them at her feet.

Since comparatively few of the sourdoughs made any gold worth mentioning (for thousands were quickly dis-illusioned) and since the men far outnumbered the women, the heady and costly joys of the glamour girls were beyond the reach of most. Consequently there was a host of camp-followers and harlots. The latter lived in Paradise Alley, where their names were blazoned over their doors, and in the tents and tin shanties of 'Lousetown', a suburb on the opposite side of the river.

There was little regular coinage in the far north, and gold-dust was the normal currency. Delicately balanced scales stood on every counter in the saloon bars and stores—a Chinese storekeeper is said to have had ivory scales—and cash-tills had special compartments for 'dust'. Underneath the sum payable on a cheque would be written the word *Dust*. Nuggets were more inconvenient, since they could not be divided up and weighed to buy goods to a specific value, whether in food, liquor, mining gear, or women, and most of them were melted down in forges in the town. So the sourdoughs returning from the desolate creeks to carouse in Dawson stuffed their pockets with gold-dust. Often they left a thin yellow powdery trail through the streets of the town, with a wake of scavengers combing the ground.

Waiters made small fortunes by sweeping and collecting all stray particles of 'dust', sometimes coating their fingers with resin the better to hold the grains. Many a sourdough was deliberately jostled and pushed in order to spill a little more of the precious dust from his pockets. Just how far this undignified behaviour went can only be imagined, and the mind builds up a ludicrous image of white-aproned, black-coated, side-whiskered waiters snooping, swooping, stooping—and brushing up. Even today workmen demolishing or repairing a Dawson building sweep into pans the dirt from underneath and between the floorboards and in every crevice and wash it. Only recently in such an operation nearly £2,000 in pure gold was scraped up. Panning mud and dirt is in the blood in the frozen north, and Dawson's streets, it would seem, are still literally paved with gold.

That some of the brash characters in saloons and dance-halls became rich without roughing it in the gold-fields is evident from the example of the Greek Alexander Pantages, who was christened Pericles but, holding that the sword was mightier than the pen, changed his name to Alexander. He was typical of the adventurers in the Yukon. As a boy he worked with his father in a Cairo restaurant and later went to sea, working his passage round the world until the chill breath of Midas drew him to Dawson. Here he became barman at the Monte Carlo, but not for long. Soon he was able to establish the Orpheum Theatre, and he set up house with Klondike Kate (without the blessing of Church or State). Ultimately he became one of the great names in American theatrical history.

In the hot-house luxury of the dance-halls champagne flowed at $30 a bottle, and gustatory pleasures were equally penalizing, with moose pies at $5 apiece, but in the hotels and bars these things were rather cheaper. There were hotels like the Yukon, Bonanza, and Occidental, and bars like the Red Feather Saloon ('Dell's Place'), the Bank Saloon, and Bill McFee's Pioneer, with its stuffed moose-heads. The dance-halls and larger establishments had gaming-rooms at the back, often with roulette tables, and here gathered the professional gamblers, conspicuous in black frock-coats, with pale hands and perhaps a toothpick in the corner of the mouth. In most of the bars, however, the tables were usually crowded over sessions of stud poker, black jack, crap, and faro.

Such things were winked at by the authorities and the law-abiding citizens, for it was, very largely, a law-abiding community. The community's own self-interest and the authority of the North-West Mounted Police combined to secure that. Inevitably there was an elemental brutality in the life of the Yukon, inevitably scoundrels and harlots were present and there was brawling and occasional gunplay. Certainly there were not the gun battles of Deadwood in South Dakota or the gambling hells and elaborate brothels of Virginia City in Nevada, centres of earlier gold booms in the American West. Soapy Smith, after all, had been driven to Skagway, and of actual crime the police records show little.

There was always in Dawson a substantial element composed of respectable professional men and traders with their wives. There were such men as Frank Foster, a Yorkshire-man who arrived in 1899 and became a trader in Fort Yukon, where his library included Demosthenes and Carlyle. There was George Black, who in 1898 came as a lawyer to Dawson City, where he remained to become Commissioner of the Yukon Territory and Speaker of the Canadian House of Commons, after having led the Yukon Infantry Company to France in 1917. There were such women as Mother Mary

Mark, Superior of the convent and hospice in Dawson, who came up the Yukon River in 1899 and was still there at the end of the last war. Even Klondike Kate, 'Queen of the Yukon' (who died as recently as 1957), was essentially good, gentler and kinder than gun-holstered Kitty LeRoy, the earlier 'Queen of Deadwood'.

There are those who say that the Klondike was tough and lawless. There are others who hold that it was all as innocent as a kindergarten. Listening today to an old phonograph in a Dawson log cabin, its tinny cracked voice playing polkas and waltzes of the 'nineties, one is almost convinced of the exaggeration of a Robert Service. The image of violence dissolves, and the mind's eye comes to hold not a Dangerous Dan McGrew or even a Soapy Smith, but rather a Charlie Chaplin or a Chester Conklin, pathetic waifs who, at last, struck a little gold and then strutted along Dawson's Front Street in stiff new hats and gaudy ties to buy an evening of oblivion in one of the dance-halls, where Spanish Jeanette or Sweet Marie was a glorious alcoholic vision, as remote and inaccessible as a goddess.

By 1901 it was all over. Dawson City blossomed and withered within the span of little more than three years. The population dropped to just over a thousand inhabitants. It became a ghost town, a mere wraith, and it has survived like that, the strangest of museum-pieces, for well over half a century. Front Street is overgrown with weed and rickety with decaying duckboards. The hotels, dance-halls, saloons, and stores are shuttered and closed tight with rusty padlocks, their original furniture and fittings still in place, mantled with dust. In empty dark hotels guest-books still lie beside scales and cash-tills with their compartments for gold-dust. In the stores there are guns, playing-cards, kitchen utensils, forgotten tins of vintage tobacco, and piles of yellowing mining-claim papers, all mouldering upon the shelves. The faded names of traders long dead still appear over many of these stores, and the name of Madame Tremblay can be discerned on the derelict shop that once supplied the ladies of the town with their glistening finery. The Klondike Nugget and Ivory Shop opens to do a seasonal tourist business in the ivory tusks of the long-extinct mastodon, dug out of the frozen ground by prospectors before the turn of the century. Beside it, in archaic glory, stands the fire-engine of 1899, still in use. Everywhere are deserted log cabins, the broken windows awry, leaning and tottering like the tipsy sourdoughs themselves.

The fabulous Flora Dora survives as the Royal Alexandra Hotel, though the original name is set in golden splendour over the entrance to the pool-room. In the saloon, where Klondike Kate and Diamond-Toothed Gertie danced on the bar, the myths of the frozen north live on in the conversation of tourists and couriers, and the flamboyant Victorian-Edwardian furniture and décor stimulate make-believe. In the entrance hall the Floradora Girls dance on in an old photograph. In the bedrooms, with the amenities that passed for *confort moderne* half a century ago, actresses of the Naughty 'Nineties smile archly from bamboo picture-frames. Elsewhere there are life-size paintings of nudes, and on the staircase is a massive 'Susanna and the Elders' of mysterious provenance. It was certainly not painted in Dawson. Was it then carried over the Chilkoot, as Mike Mahoney and Bull Ballantyne carried their pianos?

For a brief spell Dawson was the seat of the local government of Yukon Territory, but in 1950 even that honour was lost (to Whitehorse), and today Government House is still graced with state-rooms filled with chandeliers and oil-paintings, rich carpets and furniture, though no one has set foot in it for decades.

There are plans for a Gold-Rush Festival to be held in Dawson City, and some of the old landmarks are to be restored, among them the Palace and Nugget dance-halls. In the rebuilding that has already begun substantial amounts of gold-dust have again been recovered from the derelict buildings and the mud, as well as pistols, bullets, and bracelets that may once have adorned the wrists of the 'girls'. The Yukon is out to catch the 'dude hunter' market, and before long the station-wagons will be piled high with antlers and bearskins, while the sagas of Dangerous Dan McGrew and Soapy Smith will go from strength to strength in the telling. . . .

There are, however, still a few, a very few, octogenarian survivors of 1898 in Dawson who are still picking holes into the solid mountainside, still searching for the mother lode of ore, and from them it is possible to get very near to the truth about the Gold Rush.

The Social History of the Nautch Girl

BY MILDRED ARCHER

WHEN THE British went to India in the eighteenth and nineteenth centuries there was one institution about which they all had something to say. Some disapproved. Some were delighted. No one was silent. This was the 'nautch', an entertainment by professional dancing-girls who performed and sang to the accompaniment of musicians.

Sir James Mackintosh, the Recorder of Bombay from 1804 to 1811, found it insufferably boring.

It seemed to me like all the others I had seen, abominably tiresome. Nothing was ever so ridiculously exaggerated. . . . Nothing in the exhibition deserves in my opinion the name of voluptuous, in any sense of the word, pure or impure. I think it unmixed dulness.

Lady Dufferin, Vicereine of India from 1884 to 1888, was thankful when it finished.

Plain women with harsh voices sang loudly, while they gently moved backwards and forwards on the space allotted to them; they chewed pan at intervals and made faces, and no one could tell what they were singing about; and so when we had had enough we said so and the entertainment ended.

William Simpson, the Crimean War artist, on the other hand, saw the nautch in a very different light. He was admittedly under the influence of Thomas Moore's *Lallah Rookh*, for he and his military friends actually read the poems to one another as their boat glided through the pink lotuses across the Dall Lake to the gardens of Shalimar in Kashmir. And it was there, after night fell, that dancing-girls performed by torchlight. He speaks of 'the sweet delusion of a never-to-be-forgotten night'. 'The Peris of Paradise', he wrote, 'were not a matter of faith—they were realities before us.' Even the acid-tongued Emily Eden, who accompanied her brother Lord Auckland, the Governor-General, to India in 1836, said 'the whole thing was like a dream', and Mrs Elwood, who was in western India from 1825 to 1828, found it 'so completely Oriental that I only wish I had Sir Walter Scott's powers of description to give you an idea of this graceful entertainment'.

Boring or enchanting, dull or glamorous, which was right? The question is not easy to answer. Judgment depended as much on who you were as on what you saw. Were you solemnly approaching the nautch as a serious part of Indian culture or were you accepting it as a frolicsome amusement which had beguiled countless Indians, including the Mughal Emperors Akbar and Jahangir? Did you enjoy *risqué* entertainments? With Indian women normally secluded, nautch girls were clearly public women—'tolerated courtesans', as one Company servant described them. Did you have views on 'public women'?

But the nautch girls themselves and the settings in which

they performed were also influential factors. The circumstances in which the British saw them varied greatly. Sometimes the dancers appeared at the houses of wealthy Indian
gentlemen when *soirées* were given to celebrate one of the
great Hindu or Muslim festivals. At these parties the nautch
was often a background accompaniment to conversation as
couples strolled from room to room, chatting to their friends.
It was like gramophone music at a party or an orchestra in a
restaurant, and it became inseparable in the memory from
the glitter and lavish hospitality of an Indian assembly.
Mrs Belnos, who lived in Calcutta in the early years of the
nineteenth century and who published a volume of her
sketches depicting life in India, provides a vivid description
of such a party:

> On entering the magnificent saloon, the eye is dazzled by a
> blaze of lights from splendid lustres, triple wall shades, chandle
> brass, etc., superb pier glasses, pictures, sofas, chairs, Turkey
> carpets, etc., adorn the splendid hall; these combined with
> the sounds of different kinds of music, both European and
> Indian, played all at the same time in different apartments;
> the noise of native tom-toms from another part of the house;
> the hum of human voices, the glittering dresses of the dancing
> girls, their slow and graceful movement; the rich dresses of
> the *Rajah* and his equally opulent Indian guests; the gay circle
> of European ladies and gentlemen, and the delicious scent of
> attar of roses and sandal which perfumes the saloon, strikes
> the stranger with amazement; but he fancies himself trans-
> ported to some enchanted region, and the whole scene before
> him is but a fairy vision.

A similar occasion is described by Sir Charles D'Oyly, a
member of the East India Company's civil service in Bengal
from 1796 to 1839. D'Oyly was a famous wit and amateur
artist of his day and his description comes from a long
burlesque poem entitled *Tom Raw, the Griffin* (published in
1828), in which he gives a picture of the life of a newly
arrived cadet (a 'griffin') in Calcutta. Amongst his early
engagements was a *soirée* given by an Indian gentleman,
'Nob Kishen', as he calls him, to celebrate the Durga Puja
Festival in October. At a certain point during the evening's
entertainment the guests were seated, the dancing-girls and
their musicians came forward, and the display was not
unlike a private ballet in an eighteenth-century palace.

Detail from the *Akbarnama* (Annals of Akbar), *c.* 1600: Victoria and Albert Museum

The Nautch Girl

See! how invitingly the creatures dance!
What elegance and ease in every motion!
Not as the ladies do at home, or France,
So turbulent and full of strange commotion;
Of this our Indian fair have an odd notion;
Their step is slow and measured—not a caper
That lifts them from the ground,—but grave devotion
To time, and suppleness of figure's taper,
It is no doubt the modestest—at least on paper!

Or how describe the graceful play of arms,
Which, beautifully waving, as they move,
Reveals, at every step, a thousand charms;
Expressing terror, languishment, or love;
While their dark, speaking eyes, unceasing rove.

See the Circassian—'tis a pleasing sight,
With uplift arms her filmy veil is spread,
Like a transparent canopy, and light
As cobwebs on the lawn on which you tread,
Rolling from side to side her airy head
Swift as the agile roe's elastic bound;
Then, in a giddy evolution led,
Her full robes, whirling, gracefully around,
She sinks amidst her sparkling drap'ry to the ground.

Still, to the cadence of the sprightly air,
Her supple limbs and waving head she plies;
Now, drooping forward, bows with modest care;

246

This and the illustration opposite are
from Mrs Belnos' *Twenty-four Plates
Illustrative of Hindoo and European
Manners in Bengal*, 1832

Now, backward bending, flash her beaming eyes;
And, midway, now her form is seen to rise,
Till, once more, standing, she resumes the dance:
And many a varied attitude she tries,
And many a winning smile, and am'rous glance,
That—lost on us—might even Mahomet entrance!

On these occasions the dancing-girls had a varied reper-
toire of turns. Sometimes mime was employed for special
effects. Emily Eden was entranced by the 'flower dance' of
two *nautchnis* whom she saw at Benares in 1837.

One was I think the prettiest creature I ever saw, and the
most graceful [she wrote]. If I have time I will send a little
coloured sketch of her, just to show the effect of her dress.
She and another girl danced slowly round with their full
draperies floating around them, without stopping for a quarter
of an hour, during all which time they were making flowers out
of some coloured scarfs they wore, and when they had finished

Detail from a painting by an unknown Delhi artist, *c.* 1820: Victoria and Albert Museum

248

a bunch they came and presented it to us with such graceful Eastern genuflexions.

There was also the 'snake dance' when the dancers held the end of a veil in their mouths, making it look like a pipe, and then pretended to be charming a snake, swaying from side to side as though following its movements. Or else they mimed kite-flying, an amusement common in India. During this dance, as one army officer noticed, 'the heavenward direction of the eyes displays these features—as doubtless my fair countrywomen know—to the very best advantage'. Receptions of this kind were perhaps the most favourable to the performer since they provided a gay and lively background to her dancing.

But besides parties given on festival days nautch girls were often hired by Indian gentlemen to entertain some British visitor or guest of honour, and at these times the nautch girl's other role, that of singer, was equally prominent. When the guests were seated with their host, the dancing-girl would give a series of cabaret turns. Part of the time she sang a sort of recitative, suiting her expressions and gestures to the subject, showing fear, hope, love, jealousy, or despair. She would throw herself on the ground in an agony of grief or laugh with joy. The stanzas of the song would be interspersed with dancing turns, which also mimed the story. Many of those present would find it difficult to follow the songs for, as Sir Charles D'Oyly pointed out, not everyone was expert in the language.

> Few know the ditty's meaning;
> And—to speak truth, 'tis ten to twenty you've
> Not learnt the language, though—your dulness screening,
> You shout applause, as if the tongue *au-fait* you'd been in.

At parties of this kind the dancing-girl would often single out the guest of honour on whom she would concentrate her attention. She would kneel before the guest and direct her singing to that particular person. This could have ludicrous results. Emily Eden, while watching a fat nautch girl addressing Lord Auckland with meaning little smiles, asked for a translation of the song and was told: 'I am the body, you are the soul; we may be parted here, but let no one say we shall be separated hereafter. My father has deserted me; my mother is dead; I have no friends. My grave is open and I look into it, but do you care for me?' She does not record Lord Auckland's reactions.

At receptions for guests of honour, where attention was focussed on the dancing-girl, her quality was of great importance. The fee for a first-class entertainer was often very high indeed. She was sometimes a beautiful Kashmiri or Circassian with a fair skin and delicate features. She wore rich dresses—brilliant gauze skirts in red, pink, blue, or green, edged with gold or silver tinsel, over long velvet trousers or silk pyjamas. Many of the British thought the dress delightful and were incidentally impressed by its modesty. Lady Dufferin watched a girl pirouette and 'saw that she had on a regular suit of armour, cloth of gold down to the ankles. Nothing could be more strictly proper.' An army officer, Captain Mundy, also agreed that 'the dress of the Indian dancing-girl is infinitely more decent than that of our French and Italian figurantes, the long silken trousers descending quite over the feet'. Nevertheless his roving eye noticed that 'the upper portion of the costume . . . is not always quite so impervious to sight as a bodice of more opaque texture than muslin might render it'. First-class dancing-girls also wore ornaments of gold and silver. Their jewellery tinkled as they danced and Sir Charles D'Oyly, amongst others, was fascinated by its variety.

> What shall we say of nose encircling rings,
> Or the rich pendants of the loaded ear,
> Armlets, and all those curious sorts of things
> That Indian females on their persons bear?
> But chief the bells they round their ankles wear,
> That, to the motion of their well made feet,
> Jingle in cadence to the native air,
> And mark the time—now solemn and now fleet,
> As on the echoing floor they tremulously beat?

But, above all, they were trained to sing and dance with distinction. Famous nautch girls, such as Kaunum and 'Nickie', had excellent voices.

> But hark, at Nickie's voice—such, one ne'er hears
> From squalling nautchnees, straining their shrill throats
> In natural warblings, how it greets our ears,
> And brilliant jingling of delicious notes,
> Like nightingale's that through the forest floats.

From *The Costume and Customs of Modern India*, 1813

Between the verses of their songs they sailed around with 'a beautiful swan-like march' and accompanied their songs with slow and graceful movements.

Few nautchnis, however, exuded quite such glamour, and British distaste or disillusion was probably caused by the failure of dancers to maintain these lyrical standards. Ordinary dancers were often old and ugly, their clothes soiled and bedraggled with tarnished tinsel finery. And it must have been one of these that Captain Broughton watched, for she presented 'the appearance rather of an Egyptian mummy than of a living female tricked out to captivate and allure'. Cheap dancing-girls were loaded with heavy tawdry jewellery which looked barbaric. Certain of the British could

From *The Costume and Customs of Modern India*, 1813

not abide 'the massive and numerous ear-rings which dis-
figure the feature they are intended to adorn, or the heathen-
ish and unaccountable nose-ring, the use of which (for it is
certainly no ornament) it is hard to discern—unless these
dangerous sirens are furnished with them, like pigs, to keep
them out of mischief'. Their voices were harsh and untrained
and their dance repetitive and monotonous. Julia Maitland,
a judge's wife in south India in 1836 to 1839, complained of
their 'bawling like bad street-singers—a most fearful noise
and no tune', and she defied anyone 'to have watched this
girl's dull, unvarying dance long, without going to sleep'.

It was certainly a very mediocre dancing-girl whom Mrs
Fenton saw in Calcutta in 1826. This gay and flighty wife of

an army officer had made up her mind to see a nautch in spite of her husband's disapproval. But she was sadly disappointed.

Like many other Europeans [she wrote] I had a violent curiosity to see a Nautch. These native assemblies are much frequented about Calcutta, but I am told the true Hindoostanee nautch, as it is exhibited in the higher provinces, is such as no lady could witness. To *this* Fenton was extremely unwilling I should go, but all his assurances that I should be both disgusted and disappointed, failed to convince Jemima Aitken and myself, go we must and did. . . . [Her Indian host] brought forward an odious specimen of Hindoostanee beauty, a dancing woman, for my special gratification, but such a wretch—dressed in faded blue muslin bordered with silver, put on in some fashion passing my comprehension. It appeared at least twenty yards, rolled in every direction about her, the ends brought over the shoulders and hanging down before, her hair falling wild about her face. She was dressed in good keeping for a mad woman. The musicians then commenced a native air, merely a repetition of four notes; she advanced, retreated, swam round, the while making frightful contortions with her arms and hands, head and eyes. This was her 'Poetry of motion'; I could not even laugh at it. I drove home cured for ever of all curiosity respecting native entertainments.

Such experiences were common enough—especially amongst British women—and one suspects that at heart it was men only who entered into the spirit of a nautch, who were not unduly critical and whose will to enjoyment more easily transcended the dull, the cheap, or the drab. Despite their appearances in mixed society, nautch girls were primarily intended for men and it was to male company that they chiefly responded. At gatherings where men only were present they shed all stiff reserve and cool propriety and, whether plain or pretty, became new persons. The nautch lost its air of a private ballet and more nearly resembled a night-club or an American burlesque. There was much teasing and back-chat, liquor flowed and applause encouraged the performers to 'unparalleled' acts.

For the British, such gatherings were of two kinds. In many cases Indian gentlemen had separate establishments or 'garden houses', where they retired for a night's entertainment and to which male British friends were sometimes invited. At other times, British men went 'nautching' alone.

In the eighteenth century particularly, when Company servants were free and easy with their money, lonely individuals would send for nautch girls to entertain them in their own houses. More frequently, groups of civilians, or army officers living in cantonments, would club together and hire girls for an evening's amusement. So popular were these entertainments that nautchnis began to move *en masse* to the British stations. Captain Williamson noted in his *Costume and Customs of Modern India* (1813) that

> between the years 1778 and 1785, it is certain that the prime sets of dancing-girls quitted the cities, and repaired to the several cantonments, where they met the most liberal encouragement. Then the celebrated *Kaunum* was in the zenith of her glory! Those who did not witness the dominion she held over a numerous train of abject followers would never credit that a haughty, ugly, filthy black woman could, solely by the grace of her motions, and the novelty of some Cashmerian airs, hold in complete subjection, and render absolutely tributary, many scores of fine young British officers! Nay, even the more discreet and experienced, many of whom could not, with propriety, say, 'Time has not thinned my flowing hair, nor bent me with his iron hand', were found among the most fervent of the proud *Kaunum's* admirers.

At these parties the most popular dance was the *kuharwa* which Captain Broughton, Resident to the Court of Sindia in 1809, described as follows:

> When a girl is to dance the *kuharwa*, she ties a sash round her loins, through which she pulls up her gown, puts another across her shoulders, and a man's turban upon her head, and in this dress, unless she is naturally very pretty, she looks worse than before: though to a fine animated countenance it gives a certain spirited and roguish air, which seldom fails to attract a due degree of admiration. In this favourite dance the most indecent gestures are used, meant to raise admiration and desire, but which, in uninitiated English bosoms, seldom excite anything but disgust. Such attractions has it, nevertheless, that it is always called for; and young and old, great and small, Europeans as well as natives, look forward to the *kuharwa* with anxiety, and sit for hours to witness its performance.

It was no uncommon thing at these gatherings for the girls to continue dancing and singing throughout the night until daybreak. Only then would their audience return home, tired and bedraggled but delighted with the entertainment.

Ladies in the Air

BY CHARLES GIBBS-SMITH

WHENEVER WE men have tried to keep women out of some traditionally male preserve we have always had the tables turned upon us and found ourselves eating extremely unpalatable humble pie. Only in London clubs have ladies so far failed to win the day—but that day is near, too. The only thing that we can do is to face up to the fact that women, when they put their minds to it, can do almost anything as well as we can. It is particularly gratifying for feminists to find that in the ostensibly male sphere of aviation and aerostation women have been 'in it' from the start.

Ladies first mounted in the air on 20 May 1784, in Paris, when one marchioness, two countesses, and one mademoiselle went up with one marquis and one monsieur in a tethered Montgolfier balloon from the Faubourg St Antoine; but, since on this first trip the balloon was tethered, the honour of being the first member of the fair sex to make a proper aerial voyage passes to a certain Mme Thible, who in a magnificent Montgolfier hot-air balloon named *Le Gustave* rose at Lyons on the 4th of June in that same year 1784 in the presence of the King of Sweden, and flew with M. Fleurant for forty-five minutes; during which time the balloon drifted for about two miles, and the pilot and his lady sang arias to each other in the wicker gallery set around the neck of the balloon.

In 1797 the French pioneer A. J. Garnerin made the first live air-drop in a parachute from a balloon over the Parc Monceau in Paris. On 18 October 1799 the first woman descended, in the person of his intrepid wife Jeanne-Geneviève. The first professional woman pilot was Mme Blanchard, also the wife of a famous aeronaut, J. P. Blanchard, who had made the first aerial Channel crossing with Dr Jeffries in 1785. Mme Blanchard first went solo in a balloon in 1805, and was, tragically, the first woman to die in an air-crash when her balloon caught fire during a firework exhibition and crashed into a Paris street in 1819.

The first woman to fly in an aeroplane was the French sculptress Thérèse Peltier when she went for a brief spin as passenger with Delagrange in his Voisin biplane at Turin on 8 July 1908. Soon after, Mme Peltier did make a tentative solo flight, but did not qualify as a pilot. The honour of being the world's first qualified woman pilot belongs to the Baroness de Laroche, who was trained on a Voisin, and received her 'Brevet de pilote d'aéroplane' on 8 March 1910. She was badly injured in a crash in July that same year, and was killed flying in 1919. The second qualified woman pilot was the Belgian Hélène Dutrieu, the most distinguished woman pilot of her generation.

The first woman to fly in a dirigible was Mme Lebaudy in 1904, as a passenger in a Lebaudy airship. She was in fact beaten to the start by a Mme d'Acosta, who actually piloted the Santos Dumont No. 9 airship by herself for a short distance on 24 June 1903; but she was officially disallowed as having truly flown, because she had the trail-rope dragging along the ground, closely followed by a chivalrous ground crew eager to grab it in case of need!

The first British woman to fly in an aeroplane as a passenger was Miss Gertrude Bacon, who went up with Sommer in 1909; and the first British woman to become a qualified pilot was Mrs Maurice Hewlett, wife of the author, who received the Royal Aero Club's Certificate No. 122 in August 1911. The second British woman to qualify as a pilot was the beautiful Mrs Beauvoir Stocks (Certificate No. 153 of 1911), who was badly injured in a crash in 1913.

Since those early days women have proved themselves excellent pilots, and, of course, ubiquitous travellers on the airways of the world.

ROYAL AQUARIUM

ZAZEL

'An aeroplane must move swiftly to stay up in the air. The minimum speed at which an aeroplane can remain in the air depends largely upon its weight.'

—RICHARD FERRIS,
How to Fly, 1910

ZAZEL DAILY, 5.30 & 10.30.

257

'The nation's airports are already jammed; longer runways will be needed. . . . Even without the jet factor, present-day traffic control systems cannot handle the load.'

—*Newsweek* magazine, 1956

'There have always been those who look at the birds and envy them as they "sail upon the bosom of the air".'—C. H. GIBBS-SMITH, *History of Flying*, 1953

'Then the machine turned bottom upwards and rushed vertically towards the earth.'—OTTO LILIENTHAL, in *The Aeronautical Annual*, 1895

'The air hostess has attracted thousands to air travel.
Marriage claims them very fast, as records of T.W.A.
show that the average length of services is only fifteen
months.'—Trans-World Airlines press release

'I likewise desire that I may have the sole teaching of persons of quality, in which I shall spare neither time nor pains till I have made them as expert as myself. I will fly with the women upon my back for the first fortnight.'

—JOSEPH ADDISON, in *The Guardian*, 1713

'Their whole behaviour indicates that a flight like this is no labour, but rather akin to resting.'—*Aeronautical Annual*, 1897

'My only fear is that our wives will always want to be in the air with us.'
—CLAUDE GRAHAME-WHITE, in conversation, 1911

'Well,' says she, 'I have sailed, as you call it, many a mile in my lifetime, but never in such a thing as this.'
—ROBERT PALTOCK, *Peter Wilkins*, 1751

(The balloonist is the French lady, Madame Blanchard)

'A test pilot's duty is to stay in the aircraft and try to get it back in one piece, particularly if it is an experimental proto-type.'—PHILIP LUCAS (quoted by Constance Babington Smith in *Testing Time*, 1961)

(The German parachutist Käthe Paulus)

'Instruments to flie withall, so that one sitting in the middle of the instrument, and turning about an engine, by which the winges being artifici-ally composed may beate the ayre after the manner of a flying bird.'
—ROGER BACON, *The Mirror of Alchimy*, 1597

(The German aviatrix Melli Beese)

'The issue of aeronauts' certificates for proficiency in piloting balloons, including a solo voyage, was, however, refused to women on grounds that they were prone to lose their heads too easily.'

—GRAHAM WALLACE: *Flying Witness*, 1958

'It was about 12.30 in the noon hour on Thursday, 20 November, 1952, that I first made personal contact with a man from another world. He came to Earth in his space craft, a flying saucer. He called it a Scout Ship.'
—GEORGE ADAMSKI, *Flying Saucers have landed*, 1953

(The French aviatrix Hélène Dutrieu)

'What is chiefly needed
is skill rather than
machinery.'
—WILBUR WRIGHT,
letter to Octave Chanute,
1900

'I hate to shoot
down a Hun without
him seeing me, for al-
though this method is
in accordance with my
doctrine, it is against
what little sporting
instincts I have left.'
—J. B. MCCUDDEN,
V.C., *Five Years in the
Royal Flying Corps*,
1918

'Goddess with the zoneless waist, and wandering eyes, still leaning on the arm of Novelty.'

—WILLIAM COWPER, *The Task*, 1785

'Mrs Watt Smyth, the founder of the Women's Aerial League, said that their great wish was to be treated as a serious and earnest body of women working to establish aviation as a science and an industry in this country.'

—*Flight* magazine, 1910

(The Baroness de Laroche, the world's first woman pilot)

'I feel perfectly confident, however, that . . . we shall be able
to transport ourselves and families, and their goods and chattels,
more securely by air than by water, and with a velocity of
from 20 to 100 miles per hour.'

—SIR GEORGE CAYLEY: *On Aerial Navigation*, 1809

'The engine is the heart of an aeroplane, but the pilot is its soul.'
—SIR W. RALEIGH, *The War in the Air*, 1922

(World War II ferry pilot Miss Joan Hughes)

'The most attractive duck pictures are of incoming ducks flying toward the camera at low altitude.'

—EDGAR M. QUEENY,
Prairie Wings, 1947

(The English aviatrix Mrs C. de B. Stocks)

'*Cet appareil fut et est resté le plus petite aéroplane qui ait jamais porté un homme.*'—A. DUMAS, *Ceux qui ont volé*, 1909

(English aviation writer and photo reconnaissance expert, Miss Constance Babington Smith)

'I see no objection to women making space flights. A physically well-trained woman could easily stand up to the stresses and strains of such a flight.'—MAJOR Y. GAGARIN, in an interview, 1961

Crowning Glories

BY OLIVE COOK

XCEPT PERHAPS to readers of the
omen's glossies the currently occur-
ng designation 'hair artist' strikes a
retentious and faintly ridiculous note.
et the master hairdressers of the past,
éonard, Croisat, Stéphane, all looked
pon their fragile, ephemeral creations,
o often doomed to last but for a
ngle evening or at most a day, as
orks of art. And in their curious sym-
olism, reflecting as they do the moods
nd aspirations of different ages, hair
yles are as expressive as painting or
ny of the visual arts.

The very history of fashions in hair-
ressing closely parallels that of paint-
g. Just as the painter, liberated during
the Romantic period from the dis-
cipline imposed by a definite com-
mission and a distinct role in society,
gradually advanced towards a state of
anarchy and complete ambiguity, so the
hair stylist, from 1830, when M.
Croisat introduced the revolutionary
system of suiting a coiffure to the
wearer's face and bearing instead of
compelling the client's locks to assume
the contemporary mode, has become
increasingly eclectic, until today in the
course of one afternoon and with the
aid of his lacquer spray he may produce
recognizable transcriptions of most of
the coiffures of the past fifty years,
high, flat, smooth, curled, long or short.

Crowning Glories

The significance of this present state of hairdressing becomes instantly apparent when it is compared with the fashion among a people rooted in tradition, firm in their convictions, and inherently conservative. Such were the Japanese at the beginning of the twentieth century, and in his *Glimpses of Unfamiliar Japan* Lafcadio Hearn gives a detailed description of the fourteen ways of dressing the hair which were in general use at that time. These various modes were not created to suit fat, thin, round, square, or oval faces; they had evolved slowly through centuries and corresponded to the age and state of the women who wore them.

Thus the hair of little girls of from seven to eight was arranged in the O-tabako-bon or honourable smoking-box style, cut short all round and gathered up into a topknot, the shape of which suggested the odd name of the coiffure. The young girl graduated to the 'new butterfly' style, and from then until she was twenty-eight her hair was dressed in an ever more elaborate manner. As a sign of her maidenhood she retained a small shaven spot on the crown of the head until the time of her marriage when her coiffure took on its most complicated form. If she had not married by the age of twenty-eight there was only one more style for her, the *mochiriwage*, severe and plain, of the old woman.

All Japanese women had their hair dressed once in every three days, the hairdresser going from house to house at regular fixed hours. He would use many kinds of combs, fine loops of gilt thread, pieces of silk, delicate steel springs and basket-like moulds to build up the marvellous edifices of the prescribed fashions, and so that their handiwork should not be disturbed the women slept on wooden pillows.

These contrivances recall a highly stylized period in European history, the latter part of the eighteenth century when the hair, real, false, and powdered, was so extravagantly piled up as sometimes to reach a height of three feet. The coiffure was arranged over an enormous pad on which were heaped three top puffs and these in turn were surmounted by some fantastic ornament, a cluster of fruit and flowers, a trophy of arms, or even a model ship in full sail. These ponderous arrangements were the subjects of innumerable caricatures and satirical rhymes:

Crowning Glories

Muse begin the comic lay
Sing the female of today,
Sing her large terrific head;
Nor the many things disguise
That produce its mighty size;
And let nothing be forgot,
Carrots, turnips and what not,
Curls and cushions for imprimus,
Wool and powder for the finis;
Lace and lappets, many a flag—
Many a parti-coloured rag—
Pendant from the head behind,
Floats and wantons in the wind,
Many a gem and many a feather,
Choice fanago all together,
By whose wool and wire assistance,
They with honour and surprise
Strike the poor beholder's eyes;
What a quantity of brain
Must he think such heads contain.

Mme d'Oberkirch relates in her memoirs that when she was invited to a theatrical performance at Versailles she wore little flat bottles in her hair shaped to the curvature of the head and that these held water for the purpose of preserving the freshness of the flowers which crowned her coiffure. No Japanese pillow having been invented for their comfort, Mme d'Oberkirch and her contemporaries not infrequently passed the night in a chair instead of going to bed.

The element of hysteria in a convention as exaggerated as this was symptomatic of the conditions which preceded the great social upheaval at the end of the century, and it is not mere coincidence that the close, short, casual styles which followed on the catastrophe should bear a resemblance to those which became popular after the First World War. A little later on the hairdresser responded to the Neoclassic mode by inventing the Venus style and the Apollo knot, which latter M. Croisat cleverly erected into a vertical position, plain or plaited and assisted by wire frames, the loops thus formed being known as 'coques'.

It is not difficult to connect the styles which succeeded one another through the nineteenth century and the first decades of this with the social and historical events of the age. The earliest feeble movement towards female emancipation, for instance, was reflected in the change from the soft, feminine ringlets of the Early Victorian lady to the daring bang and *chignon* of the 'seventies, and the eventual triumph of this movement was, of course, celebrated by the fashion for the mannish Eton crop.

The greater number of the hair styles shown in these pages belong to the period immediately prior to that characterized by the shingle. The size and abandon of the coiffures of these opulent Edwardian beauties are what first attract the eye. They recall the large conspicuous mode of the Japanese geisha which contrasted with the smaller, neater heads of 'respectable' women. They also have a fabulous exotic quality which relates them to the tower-like fantasies of the late eighteenth century. Like them they are the excessive gestures of a civilization about to be eclipsed. They are, too, the last expressions, overwrought and theatrical, of submissive femininity. Those unconfined and rippling tresses, those heavy, accentuated braids, coils, and loops suggest delighted, willing bondage even while they mock at it; those puffs over the ears seem to guard their fair wearers from the voice of the tempter and at the same time to deride his powers of seduction.

'FAIR tresses man's imperial race insnare.'

Left: 1830 coques designed by Croisat. *Above*: bang and chignon which replaced the fashion for ringlets (*below*).

278

The puffed, piled-up Edwardian manner contrasting with the neat, though already accentuated, braids of the 'nineties (*opposite*).

The fantastic, exaggerated, bedizened modes which preceded the war of 1914–18.

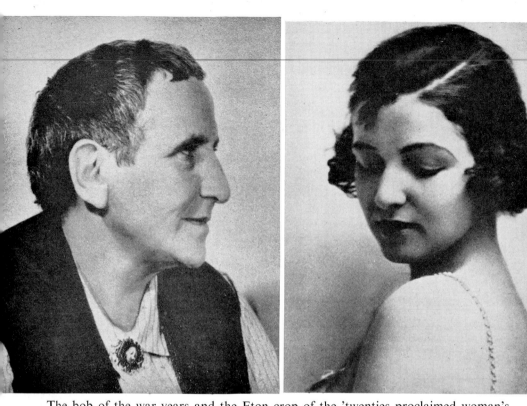

The bob of the war years and the Eton crop of the 'twenties proclaimed woman's emancipation, though coy submission was still the message of the 'earphones' (*opposite*). *Below*, a reminder of the question often asked in earlier periods: Is it her own?

PRICE LIST.

283

Hair-style of Japanese geisha, *c.* 1910

Find the Lady

BY FRED BASON

DURING 1961 I had letters from people all over the world asking me how I was getting along without Lizzie, my beloved housekeeper, who died on 1 January 1961. The flow of letters began when Leonard Russell, the former editor of this annual, wrote about my loss in *The Sunday Times*. I have no family or relations of my own. For thirty years Lizzie loved, protected and kept house for me. She was a treasure. I had had in Lizzie a very wonderful Cockney who had known me all my life and had been born and brought up in the same surroundings as myself.

I knew I would never find a second Lizzie—that was impossible. Then there is a limit to my purse-strings. I have never made more than £100 in any year from my writings. I have lived in my slum district of London all my life. So I knew it wasn't going to be easy to find anyone who could take Lizzie's place.

The first American fan-mail letter I ever got came in 1945 from New York as a result of my article in this annual in volume 5. The lady said she would like to adopt me as her 'Limey' son. She said she would like to be my ever-loving American 'mother'. I have probably received in the passing years nearly two thousand letters from her! Most of them began, 'My loving Son,' and ended 'Your affectionate Mum'.

When Lizzie died I wrote to my American 'mother', begging her to come to London for a month at my expense to look after me until I got my bearings again. I was not only heart-broken but badly crippled with sciatica. I desperately needed a little kindness—who better to ask than the woman who since 1945 had been 'my mum', who had always remembered me at birthdays and Christmas with a little gift and a card.

After three weeks' silence I got a postcard. It said: 'Quite impossible. My home is here and my niece is un-well. Good luck. Mum.' Evidently I had expected too much.

During the three weeks I waited in suspense to hear from America several women called, all willing to become my housekeeper. First there was a millionaire's secretary. She'd read about me and Liz in *The Sunday Times*. She was 'a lady', in middle life. She said that she was a little bored with mothering a millionaire. She felt that it would be rather fun to look after an author for a change. She had read *The Last Bassoon* by me, and as it was edited and intro-duced by Noël Coward she 'just knew I was all right'. (All right for *what*, she never said!) She was willing to do for me for around £20 per week, which, she said, was less than she was earning, but she was prepared to make some sacrifices.

We had our conversation in the kitchen, where the sink is in full view, and where there is *no* fridge, *no* washing machine and *no* washing-up machine. It is a cosy little room with a nice wide fireplace and comfortable chairs. I've written my article for this annual for eighteen years in this kitchen.

I said: 'You'd better see the toilet.'

I took her down into the backyard, turned to the left, and there was the door to the W.C. It was winter and it was pouring with rain.

With that she went. I never saw her again, but she wrote to me a little later asking me to go and see *her* 'little hovel'. I didn't, though I dare say she had a bathroom with all mod. con. *and* indoor W.C.

The next lady who came to see me said she'd come to try to comfort me, but she hadn't been in my home for three minutes before she herself was in tears. I got in a panic. 'For heaven's sake stop crying,' I said.

'This is my day for visitors, and if anyone comes in and sees you crying they'll think I've molested you. What's the trouble, anyway?'

The Sad Lady dried her red-rimmed eyes, refused a glass of sherry, but had some tea, and this is the story she told me:

'Oh, Freddie,' she said, 'my husband and I were listening to some gramophone records when the telephone rang. I lifted it up and a voice told me that my husband's only brother had dropped down dead in the street. I didn't know how to tell my husband, for he was an invalid and had a weak heart. But he could see the shock in my face and I *had* to tell him. We got a taxi and went to where his brother lay dead. When he saw him my husband collapsed. He lasted just a year and then he died too.'

'When did this happen?' I asked.

'Twenty-five years ago,' said the Sad Lady, weeping again. 'And you see I am still in mourning. I miss my beloved husband every day of my life.'

'But surely,' I said, 'you don't burst into tears every time you call on someone?'

'Well, Freddie,' she said, 'I *knew* somehow that I'd been down this road before. And I was coming up the stairs to the kitchen when I realized it was in this very road that my husband's brother died—and we went to see his dead body in the workhouse just a hundred yards down the road.'

Well, after that she realized she wasn't going to be much of a comfort to me, so we said goodbye, and I thought I'd never see her again.

*   *   *

The next lady to visit me was one of the most beautiful women I've ever seen. (And in my time I've known some very beautiful women, from Betty Blythe to Madeleine Carroll.) This dark-eyed, raven-haired beauty said: 'I've heard of your great loss and I'm truly sorry. I believe I am kind and warm-hearted and I'm prepared to become your housekeeper and *anything* else you like.'

I blinked, I don't mind telling you.

'I have a reason for making this offer,' she continued. 'I've two favourite writers, Somerset Maugham and you. Now for the past twelve years I've been trying to become an author as well. I've spent over £20 in correspondence courses in journalism and authorship, and I've even been to evening classes. I've written three novels and countless short stories, but everything I've written has been rejected. Everything! Not even a letter to the editor has been printed!'

'Now,' she went on, 'I want to learn the art of writing. In exchange for lessons I will look after you. I am a very good cook. I am able to do housekeeping. And if you want anything else you've only to ask. I can manage on very little. I could easily keep house on a fiver, and I am ready to move in with you next week. I have only a large suitcase.'

Did I want her? I hadn't felt in such a state for years! In a month only three people had shown a scrap of kindness to me—two Rotarians and a vicar. I was weak and ill. This time it was me who burst into tears. I don't feel ashamed of making this confession. I cried. The beautiful woman got up and came to my side, and bending over me she gave me a kiss. Then she pulled me up from my chair, put her arm round me, and said: 'It's all right—it's all right, my dear. I am here now. Your troubles are over.'

I went to the sink and bathed my eyes. Then we both had a big glass of sherry. The gods had heard my prayers. Here was a woman twenty years younger than me, and beautiful. She did not volunteer much information about her past life and I didn't ask her for any references. Her open and frank face, her lovely eyes and the condition of her fingernails were all I needed. I would take a chance on the cooking.

We had a nice tea together, and then, without me asking, she washed up. She had chain-smoked the whole time she'd been with me—very expensive-looking cigarettes of an American brand. I did wonder whether I was expected to pay the cigarette bill. Not to worry. All things would sort themselves out.

She was preparing to leave when there came a knock at the front door. I went to the door. In came the Sad Lady. I introduced the Sad Lady to the brunette, and vice versa, and said: 'Aren't I a lucky man? This beautiful lady is coming on Monday to become my housekeeper. Isn't she lovely?'

The Sad Lady looked at my new housekeeper and agreed. The brunette took her leave. I saw her downstairs and at the door she gave me a goodbye kiss. She promised to arrive about noon the following Monday.

I went back upstairs to the kitchen where I had left the Sad Lady. She had put on the kettle. After the emotional strain of the past two hours I was ready for more tea. Again I said to the Sad Lady: 'Aren't I lucky? Isn't she beautiful?'

'You must get rid of her at once,' said the Sad Lady.

I was thunderstruck. She must be either mad or jealous. 'What on earth do you mean? She is the answer to my prayers!'

The Sad Lady sat down opposite me and spoke in that sad low voice of hers: 'Freddie, someone has got to help you. I know you are a lonely man and are needing a woman. But *any* woman won't do. I am no use to you, but that lovely brunette is even less use to you.'

'Why?' I asked.

'Just look at yourself,' she said. 'You are suffering from depression and sciatica. There's barely seven stone of you, and you are over fifty years old. The woman who has just gone out is about thirty and she's full of sex-appeal. She needs a heavyweight champion, not a fly-weight like you. All that woman has got is looks. I bet she is as hard as nails when you dig the surface.'

I told her about the brunette's keenness to learn to become a writer.

'There you are,' said the Sad Lady.

'She'll learn all she can and then walk out on you. Get *rid* of her at once, Freddie. What you want is a nice quiet elderly lady to *mother* you. Don't chew off more than you can eat. You know very well you can't live on sex at your age. Now, Freddie, I've warned you. *Sleep on it.*'

I promised the Sad Lady that I would. Then from a large shopping bag she brought out a big steak, three potatoes that she made into chips, and an apple pie with superb light pastry. She cooked me a lovely supper and sat down and watched me eat it.

Next day I wrote to the would-be novelist and told her not to come on the Monday. I asked her to be generous enough to forget the whole thing for reasons that were far too involved to put down on paper. I suggested that when next she had completed a novel or an article she should send it to me and I would try to bang it into saleable shape and find a home for it —even if I had to rewrite it.

I posted the letter on the morning of the Saturday. The following Wednesday I had this letter: *Dear Freddie, I expect you are not only right but wise. Anyhow I am going to get married in ten weeks' time. I've given up the idea of becoming a novelist. I will try to become a mother instead.*

*   *   *

The next woman to enter my life was a real battle-axe.

'You want a housekeeper?'

'Yes, I do.'

'Well, you'll do,' she said. 'Hi, Harry, bring it along here!' A lorry pulled up outside my door.

'What the heck is this?' I asked.

'That's me furniture—three roomsfull of it!'

'But I have a nicely furnished home. I've got a houseful of furniture!'

'Can't be helped. Have me, have me home. I ain't getting rid of it.'

'Supposing you don't suit me?'

'Then I'll go! And I shall want me home. If you ain't got room for it

287

then it can be stored at *your expense*. It ain't coming out of my wages and that's a sure thing!'

I told her it was a sure thing she wouldn't suit me.

Then I travelled to the North of England to see a lady I'd known for some years by post. She was a very sweet lady. She would *love* to housekeep for me—but there was a fly in the ointment. Her son, aged twenty-four, was not quite certain he was in love with the girl he'd courted for four years. She couldn't leave her one and only son alone. If only he'd make up his mind then she could come to me. I gave her five days to make up *her* mind. But it was no use. The son couldn't make up *his*.

Then I called on the friendly editor of a magazine I've frequently written for, and I told him how after six months I was still alone. He said he'd help me. A week later a lady of seventy-nine came and looked after me for a little while. By chance I met the editor three or four days after the old lady had moved in. I said to him: 'I've got someone. She's seventy-nine, but doing her best.'

'Seventy-nine!' the editor exclaimed.

'So she says, and I believe her.'

'Heavens!' said the editor. 'Hope springs eternal . . .'

'What d'you mean?'

'Well, my dear chap, I couldn't think of any other way to help you so I paid £5 and had your name and full particulars put down at a matrimonial agency. If you can't find a housekeeper then you'll have to find a *wife*. But I hadn't imagined the candidate would be seventy-nine.'

Then there was the widow living in Royal Crescent who must have thought I was royalty, as she wrote to say she would like to get fixed up, and would gladly 'supervise my staff'.

And the lady who wrote that she had been a runner-up in 'Miss England' twenty years ago and still had a figure. (What figure?) And was ever so willing. (Willing for what?) And the lady in Ascot who invited me to go and be looked over with no obligation on either side. Did she think I was a horse?

And the lady who couldn't cook, couldn't sew, and was unable to scrub for physical reasons. I asked what *was* she good at, and she said: '*Conversation*'!

Life without Lizzie wasn't easy. As with so many other lonely people, I neglected myself over food. It became too much trouble to go out and get a joint of meat and vegetables, come home and cook them—and eat a real meal. I lived many days wholly on bread-and-jam, tea, and pep pills. In four months I lost a stone in weight, and the pain of sciatica increased.

Then I recorded a talk for the B.B.C. on 'Love'! I mentioned towards the end of the talk that I myself was lonely. As always, I got mail via the B.B.C. One letter struck me as being particularly genuine and sincere. It came from a lonely widow in the country. She was sixty-three. She suggested that we might meet and have a chat.

We met at Paddington Station. She had snow-white hair, rosy cheeks, a lovely smile, a merry laugh, and a keen sense of humour. Within five minutes I knew I'd found a real treasure. For a while life was rosy. I got regular meals, put on weight, and began writing my fifth diary (which Naomi Jacob had kindly offered to edit). But alas! problems arose in the lady's private life and she had to return to her home, far from London. I received her goodbye letter on 13 June—of all days! So now I'm searching again.

*   *   *

There are, it is said, 250,000 lonely widows in Great Britain. 750,000 people in England live alone. I have spent £17 on advertisements without getting any answer. Fourteen organizations have tried to find me an honest and reliable lady and failed. Eleven vicars have been asked to help and all have failed. Forty-seven readers of *The Saturday Book* have promised to keep their eyes open for a likely lady—and failed to find one.

Find the lady! Tricky, isn't it!